Reality Radio

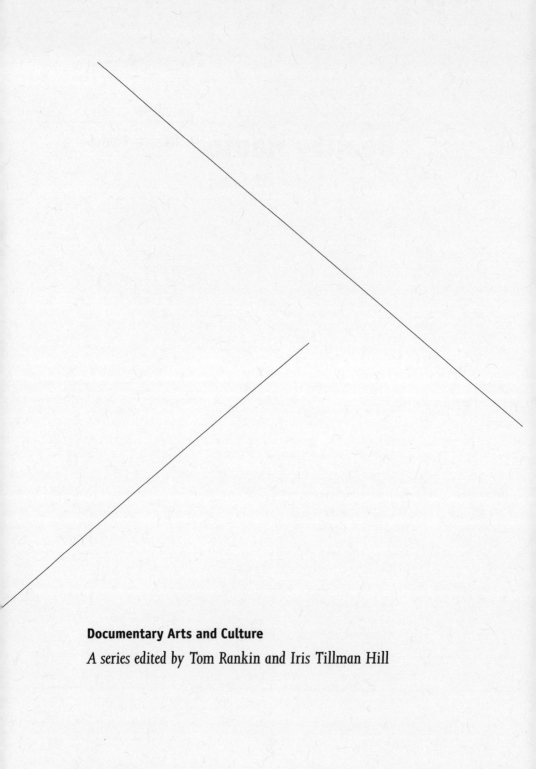

Documentary Arts and Culture

A series edited by Tom Rankin and Iris Tillman Hill

Reality Radio

Telling True Stories in Sound

John Biewen, editor

Alexa Dilworth, coeditor

Published in *Association* with The Center for Documentary Studies at
Duke University by The University of North Carolina Press Chapel Hill

DESIGNED BY BONNIE CAMPBELL
Set in Joanna MT
by Keystone Typesetting, Inc.
Manufactured in the United States of America

The paper in this book meets the guidelines for permanence and durability of the Committee on Production Guidelines for Book Longevity of the Council on Library Resources.

The University of North Carolina Press has been a member of the Green Press Initiative since 2003.

Library of Congress Cataloging-in-Publication Data
Reality radio : telling true stories in sound / John Biewen, editor ; Alexa Dilworth, coeditor.
    p. cm.
Includes bibliographical references and index.
ISBN 978-0-8078-3357-5 (cloth: alk. paper)
ISBN 978-0-8078-7102-7 (pbk.: alk. paper)
1. Documentary radio programs. 2. Documentary radio programs—Production and direction. 3. Community radio.
PN1991.8.D63R43 2010
781.44'6—DC22
2009039269

DOCUMENTARY ARTS AND CULTURE
Drawing on the perspectives of contemporary artists and writers, the books in this series offer new and important ways to learn about and engage in documentary expression, thereby helping to build a historical and theoretical base for its study and practice.

CENTER FOR DOCUMENTARY STUDIES AT DUKE UNIVERSITY
http://cds.aas.duke.edu

CLOTH 14 13 12 11 10   5 4 3 2 1
PAPER 14 13 12 11 10   5 4 3 2

For my parents,
who showed me how to listen

Contents

Foreword

Rick Moody

MY FIRST RADIO STATION, let's see. It was 1975, and I'd gone off to private school in New Hampshire. I didn't really want to go away at thirteen, because I was morbidly shy. The other kids at my school seemed to have spent their lives in private institutions and knew the sociological nuances therein. That's the back story, anyway. First day there, in the midst of a tour being given by some upperclassman, I was shunted quickly through the school radio station, WSPS. A ten-watt transmitter the size of a refrigerator wheezed in one corner. Whether the signal could reach the far end of campus was a matter of debate. Whether WSPS could broadcast to the all-important Community Center where we held dances and sold snacks was likewise controversial.

There was one studio at WSPS, which featured two old turntables, a microphone (with foam duct-taped around it to prevent the popping p's), a cart machine, and a big rack of promotional LPs yet to be stolen by the deejays. These LPs included Captain Beefheart, Nektar, and Lothar and the Hand People. The upperclassman who showed me the radio station made certain to let me know that WSPS was a campus organization that attracted the sort of people who liked show tunes. I would do better, I was told, by joining almost anything else—for example, the society devoted entirely to works of G. B. Shaw.

Instead, I was hooked immediately! Here was an art form and a discourse entirely neglected by the better part of my school, where I could work in virtual silence and exile for most of my four high school years, making perfect segues between, say, Shawn Phillips and Blue Öyster Cult, while improvising witty aperçus between the twain. Which is to say of myself and my lonely deejay friends that we liked music and art that our Grateful Dead–loving peers didn't favor. There was no danger of being interrupted in the midst of our pursuits.

What WSPS brought about in me, while we were fomenting our neglected revolution, was ear training. I suppose I had been preformatted for this, in that my family was musical (everyone could play an instrument and everyone sang) and was also interested in literature. I watched a lot of television, sure, because this was back when television was considered a fitting way to spend an entire day. I also went to the movies. But mainly what I did was: (a) sit around and listen to LPs, or (b) read books. (And for those who aren't sure what literature has to do with your ears, try reading a really bad book aloud! And then follow it up with a really good one! You will hear the difference!)

My love affair with radio continued in college. I'd risen to the ranks of program director at WSPS, and so when I went away to the Ivy League, I was primed to follow a similar path at WBRU, the Brown University radio station. And yet in the midst of my broadcasting journey something happened. There were two parallel tracks of radio at Brown, the AM track and the FM track. WBRU-FM was commercial. It actually broadcast into the city and had, therefore, a genuine playlist. In those days, a prototypical WBRU-FM band was Tom Petty and the Heartbreakers. Or maybe the Pretenders. WBRU-AM, on the other hand, was only heard on campus. (It was, I'd been told, somehow wired through the electrical system so that it was impossible to hear it anywhere else.) And so the AM format was freeform. Freeform! How the word thrilled my anti-authoritarian, would-be revolutionary heart. Accordingly, I militated for a show on WBRU-AM, where I played the entirety of *Music for 18 Musicians*, the celebrated Steve Reich composition, or excerpts from *Einstein on the Beach*. I went out to get coffee while the album sides were circumambulating.

Sadly, by my sophomore year, I was more interested in taking Quaaludes and sitting around in dorms playing that LP of T. S. Eliot reading *The Waste Land* at 45 rpm than in doing my show. Even freeform radio had become too constrictive for my tastes, or so I pretentiously argued. In the wilderness of the next years, I was a big college radio fan, always chasing the margins (New York's WFMU, of course), call letters where you were more likely to hear insects, records found in dumpsters, or free jazz than Bruce Springsteen. In my early adulthood, I found pure sound—field recordings, music from the earliest days of minimalism, and electronic music—incredibly peaceful. It would drive other people crazy but not me. I can remember, among acquaintances, more than a few who would hear what was playing in my house and ask, What the hell *is* that?

A documentary impulse was mixed up in this to some degree. I liked genuine recordings of people doing things. People frying an egg or polishing their shoes. People jumping rope or playing music on rubber bands. Or I liked music that was a variant on field recordings. Or a combination of music and sound, e.g., in Brian Eno's *On Land* or in the work of John Cage. This was as good as it got. When NPR began its relentless march into public consciousness in the eighties, I listened for political reasons, but also because mainstream radio carved people's attention down to bit-sized morsels. I was suspicious of that sort of thing. Patience is its own reward, and in the old days NPR would let the tape roll so that one's patience got a bit of a workout.

Institutions, of course, have to protect themselves. Institutions, eventually, are as concerned with their institutional continuity as they are with their nominal product. Thus, if you were a radio person in the nineties (and later, in the aughts), you both understood the will-to-rigidity of NPR and the fact that the only solution to the doldrums of radio was permanent revolution. Radio needed, and still needs, to engage with its origins in audio, if it is to innovate at all. Radio needs audio, the medium that includes sound art, documentary, collage, freeform. The medium that doesn't worry about people flipping the dial.

The essays in this book were made by people thinking with their ears. They are producers who don't go out into the world thinking about surfaces, and about how the surfaces are presented by a radio studio. Instead, these producers are listening carefully. This is a nonintrusive approach to the world, it seems to me. And though a tape recorder can be as obvious as a Hollywood cameraman on a crane, a good listener is more often in a different category entirely. Listening is receptive, unintrusive, patient.

We're in a truly liminal moment for the kind of audio that has evolved out of the freeform impulse. The bigger public radio stations, with their massive overhead, need to maximize their take, which as a practical matter has meant that certain kinds of programming have become more and more rare on the radio dial. At the same time web broadcasting, podcasting, satellite radio, etc., have made all kinds of audio much easier to produce than ever before. Technology has empowered independent producers everywhere, myself included. It's the right moment for avid listeners. There's enough good work being done out there that it's hard to keep up with it all. This is a lucky problem to have, the problem of abundance, and it is captured in these pages. Not surprisingly, these pieces, like the kinds of radio and audio they discuss, are incredibly diverse. Here's a feast! Because the way these things are discussed in these pages so much resembles what you might hear from these artists and producers on the air, the essays themselves engage your ears even as you use your eyes to read them. Which makes this a special book indeed. A book for people who care about radio and who might want to work in it themselves. Flip the page and have a listen.

Reality Radio

Introduction

John Biewen

IT WAS WAY BACK in the last century, around 1998, and some colleagues and I at Minnesota Public Radio were getting ready to launch American RadioWorks, a new documentary production unit for the public radio system. The aim was to make one-hour programs exploring issues and recent American history, with an emphasis on human stories. These programs would be distributed to stations across the country (at that time, by National Public Radio) in hopes they would broadcast them. A manager at a major station offered us some marketing advice. Whatever you do, he said, don't call these shows *documentaries*. That's instant death. Stations won't air them. Program directors will fear mass abandonment by their audiences; they'll imagine the twisting of radio dials across the land. Call it a "special," or a "special report." A "sonic extravaganza," or something. Anything but a "documentary"!

This advice was understandable, if outdated. To a lot of people back in the twentieth century, the word "documentary" evoked memories of films watched from a schoolroom desk, chin propped on folded arms, eyes glazed if open at all. The word called forth images of wildebeests teeming across the Serengeti, viewed from high above both literally and figuratively, the herd's movements described dispassionately by that Narrator with the impossibly low voice. There were other kinds of documentaries, arty or politically edgy, but only a sliver of the intelligentsia watched those.

On the other hand—staying with film for the moment—there were signs of new documentary life in the nineties. Ken Burns's *Civil War* series had drawn a stunning 40 million (voluntary!) viewers at the beginning of the decade. Michael Moore was not yet a household name, but he'd created a cult following with *Roger and Me* and the short-lived *TV Nation*.

1

On public radio, the evidence was mixed in 1998. The documentary was either dying out for good or, just maybe, beginning to blossom. National Public Radio's news magazines had once aired lots of documentary-style reporting. Sound-rich pieces up to twenty minutes long, made by NPR reporters and hosts as well as independent producers, were once a routine part of the mix on shows like *All Things Considered*. As a young reporter in the 1980s and early 90s, I'd admired and tried to emulate the work of NPR correspondents like Daniel Zwerdling and John Burnett. Their pieces had characters you could get to know, scenes you could walk into. Danny Zwerdling, though reporting from Africa, sounded nothing like the wildebeest Narrator. He was more like a somewhat nerdy friend taking you on adventures—leading you down a "narrow dirt road crowded with banana trees and children and chickens" on the way to a visit with a Zambian traditional healer. At the same time, independent producers such as Jay Allison and the Kitchen Sisters would show up on NPR with their slice-of-life pieces, usually narrated by the interviewees themselves. In 1993 *All Things Considered* broke format to air the landmark thirty-minute documentary *Ghetto Life 101*, recorded and narrated by Chicago teenagers LeAlan Jones and Lloyd Newman and produced by David Isay.

But by the late 1990s the space for such work was shrinking on NPR as the network reached for a broader audience and for more respectability as a primary news channel. NPR's talented radio makers covered the news of the day more comprehensively but told fewer intimate stories, took fewer risks, took listeners on fewer journeys. The news magazines still aired the more personal and imaginative work sent in by indie producers, but in smaller portions. The few oases in public radio expressly devoted to innovative documentary work, such as the long-running half-hour show, *Soundprint*, were often relegated to the wee hours or weekend evenings when audiences were at a low ebb.

Then again, as we got ready to hang the American RadioWorks shingle in 1998, there were stirrings in public radio at least as encouraging as in film. Ira Glass's *This American Life* had gone on the air a couple of years before. The show, produced at Chicago Public Radio and distributed by Public Radio International, was claiming ardent fans and making public radio safe again for playfulness and storytelling, at least for one hour each weekend. In New York, Dean Olsher and his colleagues at WNYC were developing an even more adventurous and eclectic show, *The Next Big Thing*, which would go live in 1999, also on PRI. In defense of our cautious public radio manager back there in '98, *The Next Big Thing* hadn't happened yet and *This American Life* was just catching on. Ira hadn't yet made even his first appearance on *Letterman*. Maybe these signs of an opening wouldn't amount to much. In the manager's further defense, American RadioWorks was going to be earnest and journalistic and not particularly hip. Perhaps he was right to be cautious.

In any case, we took the manager's advice, for a while, and avoided calling our documentaries "documentaries." The result sometimes sounded forced and downright strange, as our host served up narrative and historical docs as though they were breaking news bulletins. "This is an American RadioWorks special report: *Oh Freedom Over Me*, a look at Freedom Summer . . . Mississippi, 1964." Within a few years, though, we left such timidity behind. We brought out the "D" word and even waved it around some. It had become clear that we could proudly declare ourselves documentary makers. There was something in the air—in the broader culture, and in public radio in particular.

"We are living in the golden age of radio documentary," Samuel G. Freedman wrote in *USA Today* at the end of 2003. The Columbia University journalism professor called the flourishing of the public radio documentary "one of the most significant cultural developments of . . . the past decade."

Bold claims, given that radio itself is often seen as obsolete except as a broadcast jukebox. But Freedman was right. Over the last couple of decades, a growing corps of radio makers has transformed nonfiction audio storytelling into a strikingly vibrant form of creative expression. In 2001 WNYC followed up on *The Next Big Thing* by launching an arts show, *Studio 360*, that sometimes runs inventive documentary-ish pieces. *Radio Lab*, WNYC's electrifying series hosted by Jad Abumrad and Robert Krulwich, emerged in 2005.

Here in the twenty-first century, the word "documentary," at least to public radio listeners, has come to evoke something other than sonic brussels sprouts. It's come to stand for something almost cool.

More evidence: The radio documentary has its own festival. Each October since 2001, several hundred people converge on Chicago for the Third

Coast International Audio Festival. Third Coast is Sundance with no pictures, and the audiophiles who gather there like it that way. Plenty of us at Third Coast have gray hair (I still think of mine as "premature"), but the festival draws enough people under thirty to make an NPR exec salivate. Would-be audio producers, from teenagers to retirees, are buying recorders and microphones and making pieces of their own—for radio, for online venues like Transom and Public Radio Exchange (PRX), and for a proliferating array of podcasts. I know: I've taught a few hundred of these impassioned new producers at the Center for Documentary Studies. People with day jobs outside of radio have formed listening lounges across the country where they share their work with one another.

Reality Radio celebrates and explores this generation of audio documentary work. We at CDS invited nineteen of the most accomplished and innovative radio makers working in the English language to take us on journeys inside their heads. In these essays, documentary makers tell us—and show us, through detailed examples and transcripts—how they make radio the way they do, and why.

I feel sure that these essays have much to teach would-be radio makers, but they are more personal than theoretical, more inspirational than instructional. This book is designed for anyone who loves radio and would enjoy hearing from masters of the craft.

Stylistically, these producers are all over the lot—by design. Some are famous, some are not. The point of Reality Radio is not to canonize. The goal is to bring together producers with distinctive, powerful, and richly varied approaches to their craft. Some of our essayists call themselves audio artists. They push the boundaries of journalism to the breaking point —okay, beyond the breaking point—in the service of an aesthetic vision but also in pursuit of a different (higher?) sort of truth. Others describe themselves primarily as storytellers, drawing mainly on the narrative power of the spoken word. Still others see themselves as journalists; on the surface, at least, they emphasize information over formal innovation. But the journalistic documentarians, too, give careful attention to form and, in fact, employ plenty of (conventionally sanctioned) artifice along the way.

Some of these contributors appear in their works as narrators while others rarely put their voices on the air, but that binary distinction hardly does justice to the varying roles that these producers play in their pieces—

as explainers, facilitators, characters, performers, behind-the-scenes cho-reographers, puppet masters. Yet again, what's most distinctive about several of the essayists is their relationship to their characters—their subjects, or interviewees. We hear from the producer who mastered the "radio diary," a former reporter turned neighborhood activist who is now a character in her own stories, and a performance artist who presents her "unwitting collaborators" with loaded situations and then secretly records their reactions.

For all their diversity, these audio journalists/artists all fit within the big, stretchy tent that is documentary radio. By which I mean, they use sound to tell true stories artfully.

IN THIS POSTMODERN AGE, we're supposed to understand that there is no absolute, objective truth "out there"—certainly not one that we can vacuum up through a microphone, assemble into a perfect bundle of sonic reality and transmit to the listener. Every choice the producer makes is subject to dispute, from where to point the microphone to the digital slicing of a phrase at the expense of some nuance. The Fox News slogan, "We report. You decide," is nonsense. To report is to decide, and decide, and decide. These radio makers understand that. Few if any would claim that they're in the capital-T Truth business. But you'll notice that, almost to a person, they describe their radio work as a means of reaching for something true, of capturing human experience in the most palpable way they know how. In fact, our essayists argue that it's the very subjectivity of their work—the editing of words into "poetry," the manipulation or even manufacturing of sound, the synthesis of chaotic material into a cohesive idea, even the injection of pure fiction—that allows them to say something important, to achieve something closer to the "real." The embrace of the subjective is part of what distinguishes this work, which I'm broadly calling documentary radio, from conventional news.

But that's not all that distinguishes the two.

News, by and large, focuses on the actions of the powerful and the famous. It delivers facts about politics and war and public policy debates. The work of these radio documentarians, by contrast, tends toward the intimate, the small scale. Even when exploring Big Stories—war, the AIDS epidemic—the best radio documentaries gravitate toward the close-up portrait. In a medium that relies entirely on sound, the work explored here is often surprisingly quiet in spirit. What Bill McKibben wrote of *This American Life* could be said of much documentary radio these days: "It takes as its beat, well, life." Certainly this has something to do with the medium and its strengths—and its weaknesses. Radio does not do grand opera the way film does (or the way opera does). What it does extraordinarily well is tell stories, especially, perhaps, stories that explore the space between the ears.

The stories described here also display a distinctly populist, democratic impulse. Sometimes that impulse takes an explicit form, as when Katie Davis tells stories about the marginalized teenagers in her Washington, D.C., neighborhood or Joe Richman hands a tape recorder to a young South African woman with HIV. As often as not, though, this populism expresses itself implicitly, through attentive rendering of the "ordinary" human story.

Populism suits radio, a medium whose field equipment is inexpensive and, these days, practically as portable as a pencil. The development of cheaper and smaller recorders has fueled, or at least abetted, an important trend: some contemporary documentary producers, including many in this book, go to great lengths to get out of the way of their subjects, to let people speak for themselves and tell their own stories. That was less feasible in the first golden age of radio, when cylinder recorders filled the trunk of a car and weighed upward of a hundred pounds. These were not recorders you could carry to an upstairs apartment, let alone mail to a prison inmate with the instructions "Record yourself and send me the tapes." Back then, "documentary" producers tended to make their shows entirely in the studio.

We Hold These Truths, the landmark 1941 paean to American democracy by Norman Corwin, climaxes in a string of quotations by the "people," the "great custodians themselves." Yet the words of the office clerk, autoworker, "Okie," "mother," and "worshiper" were read by Hollywood actors such as Lionel Barrymore and Walter Brennan and apparently written by Corwin himself. Jimmy Stewart narrated the show. Corwin's genius stands, but today a producer would go out and record actual autoworkers and mothers and might also, for good measure, make them the only narrators of their stories. Other contemporary radio makers tell their own stories, or at least include themselves as important characters, dispensing not with the narrator but with the narrator's traditional detachment.

These trends toward the DIY documentary and the self-narrated story are important innovations in pursuit of an old, old impulse—to explore human experience in all its naked complexity. These radio producers often follow their characters over time. They allow them to express complete, complex, even contradictory thoughts. They plant themselves in a place and observe, peeling back layers rather than flitting over surfaces. Instead of venturing into the world and "reporting back," these producers seek to take the listener along. Whether it's a two-hour special or a four-minute slice of life, a documentary takes longer to make than a news story. And sounds like it.

Reading these essays reminds me of something a man named Robbie Osman said to me years ago. Osman was one of the white college students who volunteered to spend the summer of 1964 in Mississippi, risking his life alongside black civil rights workers to register black voters in what would come to be called Freedom Summer. Thirty years later Osman told me of his reaction that June when he heard that three civil rights workers had disappeared in Neshoba County, Mississippi. White men had long killed black Mississippians with impunity and hardly any reaction from the federal government. This time, though, two of the disappeared were middle-class white men from the North, so the response of the nation was swift and dramatic. President Johnson sent in the National Guard to search for the missing men. The news media swarmed over Neshoba County. As a young political activist, Osman had understood better than most that white lives counted for more than black lives in the United States. Some vague version of that understanding had propelled him to become a Freedom Summer volunteer. Still, the reality struck him in an entirely new way in June 1964. Here he was, breathing Mississippi air and watching this powerful reaction to the murder of two white New Yorkers just like him, while surrounded by black Mississippians whose brutal deaths would have prompted a national yawn. He found himself embarrassed at his capacity for "forgetting or underestimating" the depths of white supremacy, not just in the South but in the very marrow of the nation. "It's not that I didn't know it," he said. "It's that I didn't *feel* it."

With their varied approaches, the contributors to *Reality Radio* all seem intent on making their listeners feel something. It's not enough for them to convey facts. They gather words and sounds and music, and assemble them, painstakingly, into an *experience*.

Rick Moody is right: the producers who describe their work in these pages are listeners. They are also artists—that is, constructors of the aural realities they present. The essayists in *Reality Radio* compare their work not only to cinema but also to poetry, musical composition, even dance. "Sounds on their own aren't enough," as Alan Hall puts it. "They need a composer, a producer, a feature maker." If the radio maker does his job well, Hall adds, "a kind of alchemy takes place, a transformation of base materials into gold."

The Essays

The essays in *Reality Radio* constitute, for me, a rich and compelling conversation. It begins and ends with two people who have vastly different relationships to radio, at least on the surface. Rick Moody, whose foreword you've just read, is best known as one of our most important contemporary novelists, but he started doing radio at boarding school and hasn't stopped yet. The book's afterword is by Jay Allison, a self-described lifer who has devoted several decades, so far, to leading public radio into new and more adventurous territory. In the essays in between, you'll notice recurring and overlapping themes but also vast differences in approach, motivation, and technique. These radio makers do not occupy distinct genres, so I've made no effort to categorize the essays as if they did. That doesn't stop me, however, from seeing some broad affinities and associations among them.

The dictionary here on my computer defines a documentary as "a movie or TV program presenting facts and information, especially about a political, historical, or social issue." Even if you slip in "radio" alongside "movie or TV program," the definition is far too cramped to capture the spirit of the work described in this book. As you'll see, a number of these radio makers explicitly reject the notion that their primary job is to present "facts and information." But I'll begin my summaries with a few producers who do put that imperative front and center.

Maria Martin has things she wants you to know, people about whom she wants you to care. She produces documentaries about Americans and Latin Americans struggling with poverty, injustice, and the aftermath of war. Her work places her squarely in the century-old tradition of the social documentary. But Martin infuses her documentaries with scenes and sounds and storytelling. Given that she's often working with interviews recorded in Spanish, she takes special care to let her characters speak for more than the customary few seconds before fading their voices under the English translation. Martin wants you not only to understand the people in her stories; she wants you to hear them.

Stephen Smith wants you to hear history. My former colleague at American RadioWorks makes excellent pieces across a broad spectrum. He produced an aural portrait of the playwright August Wilson; he uncovered war crimes in Kosovo. Some of his best documentaries, and those he most loves to make, explore twentieth-century history. Smith traces the short life story of recorded sound, this magic we take for granted. And through his own pieces, like "Song Catcher, Frances Densmore of Red Wing"; "Remembering Jim Crow"; and "The President Calling," Smith shows how radio can blast us into another time, "past the rope line of textbook history."

Sandy Tolan travels the globe recording voices that Americans rarely hear, from the Mexican border to the Amazon to the Israeli coastal plain. He's determined to tell compelling human stories, those that have gotten under his skin and will get under yours. As a journalist, he also wants those stories to touch on broader issues that should demand our attention. That means that casting characters is an important part of his work. He tells us how he does it.

Radio Lab, from WNYC, has stuff to tell you, too, but goes further than any other show in combining information with wild invention. With co-host and radio legend Robert Krulwich, producer Jad Abumrad takes listeners on sonic adventures into big questions: What is morality? How do the mind and body talk to one another? Why do we sleep? Through an annotated transcript, Abumrad reveals his kitchen-sink approach to radio making. Take interviews and recorded sounds; stir in sound effects, music, elements of radio drama and sonic surprises; and infuse it all with a sense of intelligent wonder. It's a mix of learning and entertainment that has earned Radio Lab a legion of devoted fans.

The very notion of a radio documentary fan would have sounded weird at one time. The producers who have done the most to change that, and to prompt talk of a new golden age, are the masters of the personal narrative. Several of our essayists have been at this for decades, but Ira Glass created a show devoted to the narrative with a distinctly urban, and urbane, sensibility. As Glass makes clear, every story on *This American Life* has a point, a "moment of reflection," a larger meaning of some sort. But rarely is the meaning tied directly to politics or public policy. More often, the stories lead to epiphanies of the sort found in literature or the most cerebral standup comedy. In his essay, Glass recounts how he evolved from NPR reporter to the impresario of *This American Life*, and describes with detailed examples how he hears and reassembles stories.

Like Glass, Davia Nelson and Nikki Silva, better known as the Kitchen Sisters, tend to find their subjects in the everyday. They sit for hours, practically in the interviewee's lap, listening intently for those moments when speech sparkles with life. They haunt hidden kitchens and Tupperware parties, or gather lost and found sound, then create tapestries of voice, ambient sound, and music. Silva and Nelson write of radio's power to foster human connection. Provocatively, they describe their relationships with their subjects as "a sort of ventriloquism—we speak through other people and other people speak through us."

The Kitchen Sisters talk of making cinematic radio, and of being inspired by documentary film. So does Scott Carrier—who also, not incidentally, tells of being influenced early on by the Kitchen Sisters. But, despite his initial urge to do cinéma vérité, Carrier instead found himself in radio, relying mostly on his writing and his own arresting voice. "People liked my narration better than the tape," he writes with a hint of resignation. Often, for Carrier, the best way to create cinéma vérité in sound, to show the listener what he wants them to see, is to "narrate the part of the camera."

Scott Carrier, the Kitchen Sisters, and Ira Glass are familiar names to public radio listeners in the United States. Chris Brookes is much less so, unfortunately. He's one of four *Reality Radio* essayists who make brilliant radio outside the United States—in Brookes's case, from his home on the coast of Newfoundland. He conjures masterful "features," mostly for the Canadian Broadcasting Corporation. "Feature," as the word is used in Canada, Australia, and Europe, refers to a radio genre more boldly artistic than anything regularly heard in this country. Brookes writes of trying "not to *explain things* but to give listeners bits of a puzzle that . . . come together later." In that spirit, he makes dazzling use of the fluttering of a bird's wings.

Like Brookes, all of our other non-U.S.-based contributors seek mainly to engage the imagination. They're far less interested in straightforward explaining or informing. They build their pieces using the traditional raw materials of radio journalism: facts, interviews, recorded sound. But what they do with that stuff! Alan Hall, a London-based freelancer who makes features for the BBC, is a trained composer who brings a consciously musical sensibility to his radio features. For him, the grince of a flicked cigarette lighter, appearing repeatedly in an audio portrait of a former Iraq War soldier, can serve as a powerful, musical pulse, freighted with meaning. Some of those meanings can be articulated, some only felt. Hall wants to use sound to "drill bore holes into the deeper recesses of consciousness."

The Sydney-based Sherre DeLys makes a point of bringing no consistent bag of tricks to her projects. She approaches each as an "improvised, open-ended dialogue with [her] subject." You never know what approach she'll take, and neither does she, but the result is often breathtaking. DeLys ends one piece, about the late artist Derek Jarman and his seaside home, with six minutes of wordless sound: waves pulling at the shore, gulls, a bell, an electric piano. This dance of pure sound, she believes, can mesmerize us into a "slower, stiller mode that promotes reflective inquiry."

A few pages ago I wrote of producers pushing beyond the boundaries of journalism. I was mainly thinking of Natalie Kestecher. Another Australian feature maker, she records interviews and combines them with music —and sometimes mixes in fictional fables that she writes and narrates. It's "easier for me to create characters than to find them," she says. Any news director would (rightly) spew coffee across the newsroom if a reporter said such a thing. These pieces of Kestecher's are not strictly documentary—not everything in them is factually true—but we chose to include her in *Reality Radio* because she stirs her fables together with traditional interviews, thereby putting audio nonfiction to strikingly creative use. She is not trying to pass off fiction as fact. Her work is not fraud. It's art.

Dmae Roberts, of Portland, Oregon, is both artist and journalist and one of our more versatile producers. Her work has ranged from the experimental and nakedly personal ("Mei Mei: A Daughter's Song") to the sweeping historical documentary (*Crossing East*), with many stylistic stops in between. No matter the subject matter or the genre, an essential part of her work is the same: selecting and pruning the spoken words of others to "find the poetry," as Roberts puts it. In "Mei Mei," though, she helps to *create* the poetry. Roberts's Taiwanese mother, in telling of being sold as a young child, struggles to express herself in English. So Dmae writes simple, poetic lines paraphrasing her mother and hires an actor to read them. She tweaks reality in pursuit of a truer portrait. It's an act of radio craft, and of love.

These radio people, you see, do not simply hold microphones in front of people and ask questions. They get tangled up with their subjects in all kinds of ways.

Joe Richman is best known for perfecting the "radio diary." He gives people recorders and asks them to tape themselves as they go about their lives, talk with their friends or lovers, or sit on the bed at the end of the day and think out loud. Richman gets these recordings in the mail and crafts some of public radio's most memorable portraits. In thumbnail descriptions his characters may sound like victims: the teenager with Tourette's, the young woman dying of cystic fibrosis, the South African woman with HIV. But thanks to Richman, millions of NPR listeners have come to know people like Josh Cutler, Laura Rothenberg, and Thembi Ngubane as flesh-and-blood forces of nature.

Richman hands over the microphone. Katie Davis punches a different sort of hole in the traditional wall between reporter and subject. In her *Neighborhood Stories*, she does not simply document the lives of teenagers in her Washington, D.C., community. She's active in their lives, and they're an important part of hers. She runs youth programs and acts as mentor and sometimes surrogate parent to neighborhood teens. In her *Reality Radio* essay, Davis tells the story of how she came to make pieces about those teens and, often, about the lessons she's learned from them.

Out on the other coast, Portland-based damali ayo turns on her recorder as she confronts her interlocutors with performance art. She asks paint store employees to match her brown flesh tone. She sits on the sidewalk and collects reparations for slavery, handing over any contributions from whites to equally surprised blacks. As you might imagine, interesting things get said along the way. After ayo has secretly taped that dialogue, producer Dmae Roberts turns those recordings, and ayo's reflections on them, into radio. It's anything but conventional journalism, but ayo firmly believes she's delivering the news.

Dmae Roberts and damali ayo came together to make those pieces for *Studio 360*, ayo bringing the conceptual art and the recordings, Roberts the radio chops. All documentary work involves collaboration of some sort. At the very least, the producer needs the person on the other side of the microphone. Almost every audio work described in these pages was shaped and fine-tuned with the help of an editor. Many producers work with favorite studio engineers who act as a "second set of ears" and help to clean up bad recordings or execute that perfect crossfade. Producers work with other producers, whether in regular partnerships or on individual projects. Emily Botein is a full-time radio collaborator. As senior producer for *The Next Big Thing*, she helped to create many of the show's most inventive pieces with host Dean Olsher. She orchestrated the show's partnerships with artists like Rick Moody and Sherre DeLys. Since *The Next Big Thing* went off the air in 2006, Botein has worked with a variety of producers for a range of shows, including *All Things Considered*, *Studio 360*, and *Weekend America*. With Jay Allison, she co-curated the 2007 series *Stories from the Heart of the Land*. Botein "came to radio through food." In her essay, she offers a delightful comparison of her work in radio with that of her former life as a sous chef.

Through the years, a lot of documentary makers have talked about "giving voice." Giving voice to the disadvantaged, the voiceless, one's fellow man or woman. But what of the child? And what if giving voice means putting the tools of production in the hands of a teenager—all of the tools, including the director's chair? As part of this recent flowering of audio documentary work, dozens of teen radio programs have sprouted across the land, from Youth Radio in Berkeley to Blunt Radio in Portland, Maine.

Lena Eckert-Erdheim was fourteen when she became a founding member of the Youth Noise Network in Durham, North Carolina. In her essay, she takes us behind the curtain of her best piece so far: "Dressy Girls," a vivid exploration of teenage girls who wear revealing, or "skanky," clothes. As a teen interviewer, Lena elicits frank remarks from her schoolmates. Just as important, though, it's Eckert-Erdheim's story. She sprinkles the piece with incisive and funny reflections on the choices that she and her very different peers make about how to dress themselves. It's a piece no adult could have made.

Karen Michel is a gifted and accomplished radio maker in her own right, but for *Reality Radio* we asked her to write about her years of work guiding teen radio makers. Teens really are different from you and me, Michel explains. And they can teach us aging radio makers a thing or two. But that's not the reason to listen to them. Their priority, in any case, is not to educate grownups. They just want and deserve to be heard.

Oh, to be heard. And to listen.

Finally, we listen to Jay Allison. If this golden age of documentary radio can be said to have a godfather, it's Jay. He was there at the beginning, in the 1970s. He's shown the way with his own inspired work. He's encouraged, collaborated with, and convened hundreds of other radio makers. In his concluding essay, Allison tells his own story, how he went from a child with "nothing to say" to a life spent making radio. He offers reflections, his and others', on story and sound. Why do we need stories? And why this special power of stories told for the ear and only the ear?

Stories told in the dark, I like to call them. It seems fair to say that the first documentaries were stories told around the fire—long before the invention of the camera, the tape recorder, film, even the written word. Sad stories, funny stories, stories of the hunt, stories of journeys. From the mouth to the ear, with the pictures formed in the imagination of the listener. Of the modern media, radio comes the closest to that primordial form of storytelling. In conjuring rather than displaying pictures, radio is a closer cousin to the printed word than to film or television. But radio makers bring something that you can't put on a page: *sound*. The sound of life happening, the sound of the human voice. "A voice can sneak in, bypass the brain, and touch the heart," Allison writes.

It's been my honor and pleasure to work with these radio makers, coaxing them to articulate on the page what they do with sound. They've done so in compelling, entertaining, and artful ways.

Are We on the Air?

Chris Brookes

THERE IS ONE FEATURE that distinguishes me from other radio makers: geography. I am the only one whose production studio is located on the cliff where radio, as we know it, was born.

Long-distance radio transmission was delivered into the world at the top of my cliff in 1901 when Guglielmo Marconi received the first transatlantic radio transmission. So a century later when I sit down to my Pro Tools editing screen I'm conscious of the fact that two hundred feet above me is where Marconi did it, and on a foggy day all I have to do is look out my studio window to see his ghost. I like to think that this shapes my understanding of radio. It is a humble understanding, since my studio is only at the bottom of the cliff, not at the top.

Marconi spent three windy and freezing December days at the top of Signal Hill, St. John's, Newfoundland. He flew a kite to get his antenna up, glued his ear to a set of headphones, and listened for a signal transmitted from a huge spark-gap transmitter he'd built in Cornwall. He heard it, or at least he said he did. The signal was the Morse code letter "s," just pure binary information over the radio: three dots. And from my vantage point at the bottom of the cliff it seems to me this might explain why radio has been too often mistaken as a medium for information instead of evocation. Let me explain.

The important thing about the birth of radio on Signal Hill is that it didn't really happen. A physicist at Canada's National Research Council, Dr. John Belrose, has proved that it was scientifically impossible for Marconi to have heard his signal. He says Marconi had three strikes against him.

Strike one had to do with the frequency of Marconi's transmission. Shortwave radio can be received over long distances because the signal bounces off the ionosphere—particularly at night, which is why of an evening you might hear Radio Moscow in New York. But Marconi's transmitter two thousand miles away in Cornwall wasn't shortwave; it was broadcasting in the low-frequency radio spectrum. Frequencies at the low end of the dial tend not to bounce, and consequently don't travel very far.

Strike two had to do with the time of day. Marconi claimed to have received the signal not at night but at noon. The ionosphere is not particularly active during daylight hours. Finally, ionospheric reflection can be influenced by sunspot activity. More sunspots enhance reflectivity; fewer sunspots diminish it. On December 12, 1901, there was unusually low sunspot activity. Strike three.

Marconi's signal could not have bounced, and it could not possibly have been heard over the curvature of the earth two thousand miles away in St. John's, Newfoundland. Dr. Belrose knows this in the twenty-first century, but nobody knew it in 1901. Back then people had never heard of the ionosphere. They were just trying to figure out how this new radio thing actually worked. Before they managed to do that, Marconi accidentally upped his frequency a couple of years later and lucked into successful transatlantic communication using shorter wavelengths at night. Very serendipitously for him.

But on that December day in 1901, if he couldn't have heard the signal at the top of my cliff, why did he say he did? It may have been a lie, and in 1901 some said as much. Alexander Graham Bell claimed it was a hoax. These days, Jack Belrose is more charitable. He points out that Marconi had so much riding on it. He was under huge financial pressure—building the transmitter had practically bankrupted his company—and if he didn't get a signal across the Atlantic he would be finished. Dr. Belrose thinks he wanted it so desperately that he imagined he heard the signal. And he suggests this speaks to Marconi's delicate state of mind and finances at the time.

Dr. John Belrose is a scientist. I'm a radio feature maker, and it suggests something more intriguing to me, something about the essential nature of radio: that compared to other media like print or even television, radio isn't the ideal way to convey information. A radio journalist who has to do a story about economics, for example, has his work cut out for him. Readers can plow through the same story in a newspaper, and when they get muddled they can go back and reread the facts and figures until they understand them. Television viewers can see graphs and pie charts. In radio, it goes by your ears once, and if you didn't get it, too bad.

What radio does best is stimulate the imagination. And we should have realized this in the very beginning. After all, the first of our senses to develop is that of hearing. Lying in the darkness of the womb at first we can only hear. We can tell there's something out there—it may be Mom playing Mozart to us with headphones on her belly or having a shouting match in the kitchen with Dad—but we can't see it or smell it or touch it or taste it. We don't have those senses yet. All we can do is listen, and imagine what it might be. Does this hotwire a primal connection between our hearing and our imagination?

I don't know, but I do know there was this little Italian man on top of my cliff a hundred years ago, freezing his arse off in a drafty little shack, listening for three solid days with earphones clapped to his skull. A man giving radio his full attention. Does it give him the information? No. It engages his imagination so powerfully that he *imagines* the information. To me, this illustrates that radio excels not by delivering information (in this case the letter "s") but by evoking the imagination (the *suggestion* of the letter "s"). For radio program makers this should be a crucial difference.

Unfortunately on December 2, 1901, the headlines were: MARCONI RECEIVES RADIO SIGNAL! not MARCONI HAS EVOCATIVE RADIO EXPERI- ENCE. So we got off on the wrong foot. At least, that's my story, and I'm sticking to it.

In 2001, I was commissioned to produce a fifty-minute historical fea- ture to mark the centenary of Marconi's achievement. I didn't want to start off like a newsreader announcing headlines. I wanted to be more like a man selling dirty postcards. I wanted to whisper, to suggest delicious mys- tery, to entice. Since this story will climax with its central character on Signal Hill listening with a desperate intensity, I wanted to pull listeners closer to their radios from the beginning.

The program starts with a kind of *on the air* sound. I didn't use real radio static for this. We're used to static now, in our twenty-first century. Back then, almost no one was—except for Marconi and a few other experimen- ters. It was a completely new sound. I wanted a sound that modern lis- teners wouldn't take for granted. After all, back in Marconi's day they talked about the *ether*. Early experimenters believed this to be the invisible substance that conducted radio waves. It didn't exist. But if it did, I won- dered, what would it sound like?

So I tried to find sound that *suggested* the way that radio static would have struck the ear a century ago. I combined a few things and came up with something I hoped conveyed a presence, like "on." Over that bed sound I then tried to layer something to suggest a fleeting signal. I'd been to Bologna, Italy, gathering interviews and sound. Bologna was where Marconi grew up, and I'd tried to open my ears to the sounds he would have heard. In the early morning hours at my hotel, pigeons would gather on the adjoining rooftop, and I would lie awake listening to the feathery swishing of their wings cutting the air as they got airborne. A fluttering at the window was the way I imagined that the idea of radio could have fluttered at Marconi's mind, a faint signal trying to come in. An urgency. So I sneaked a stereo mic onto the window ledge and recorded the flutters. In the mix I processed the sound and pushed it into deep reverb to make "ether flutters," then slowly pulled it out of reverb to make it recognizable as wings when the program later mentions carrier pigeons.

I became fascinated by an old stone structure in the Piazza Maggiore near Marconi's birthplace. Couples would stand at different corners speaking softly into the masonry, their words reflected and focused by the roof construction to be clearly heard at the opposite corner. This was so different from my home city, whose wooden structures didn't "transmit" sound this way. I wondered if the architecture of his neighborhood could account for Marconi's obsession with signal transmission. It seemed pedantic to explain this with a script, so I teased some sound into the opening hoping it would be recognized when the full scene appeared in the program later on. I tried to use sound as enticement rather than as simple illustration. Often I cut it hard on and off to suggest nineteenth-century binary signaling.

Likewise with my script, I tried not to *explain things* but to give listeners bits of a puzzle that would come together later. To avoid a standard full-frontal narrator, I wrote a long list of questions and partial phrases that I asked an actor to read, then alternated her voice with mine. I used pauses —I think a pause allows the picture to develop in the listener's mind like a photograph slowly emerging in a darkroom chemical bath. This must not be a passive process. The beauty of radio is that the listener actively creates his or her own images with our help. For this reason it's vital to leave space in a program: room for the listener to walk in and take part.

This is the opening:

SOUND: An electric "on" bed noise that continues. An ether flutter.

VOICE: Are we on the air?

SOUND: Another ether flutter.

[pause]

VOICE: Are we on the air now?

BROOKES [recorded in Bologna's Piazza Maggiore, hard cut in and out]: Can you hear me?

[pause]

VOICE: On. The. Air.

BROOKES [recorded in the piazza, hard cut]: Can you hear me now?

MARCONI [archival recording]: Can you hear anything?

SOUND: An ether flutter.

[pause]

VOICE: What is "on . . . the air?"

HISTORIAN [interview clip]: Well you see, the first actual communication was when one person spoke to another person and they understood what they were saying, and then it goes on for thousands if not hundreds of thousands of years.

VOICE: Call. Response. Transmit.

BROOKES [recorded in the piazza]: Hello.

VOICE: Can you hear?

BROOKES [recorded in the piazza]: Hello.

VOICE: Can you hear me?

BROOKES [in the piazza]: Can you hear me?

MARCONI [archival clip]: Can you hear anything?

BROOKES [in the piazza]: I can hear you.

SOUND: Distant woman's reply recorded in the piazza.

VOICE: Receive.

BROOKES [in the piazza]: What happens if we whisper? [whispering:] Can you hear me now?

VOICE: "s"

BROOKES [in interview]: Why did they choose that?

CURATOR: Well, they used the letter "s" because they thought if they used anything with dashes in, they thought that the dots and the dashes would run into each other. And therefore the easiest letter to distinguish was "s," which is in Morse code three dots.

MARCONI [archival clip]: The letter "s."

VOICE: Sssssssss.

[pause]

VOICE: S for silence.

SOUND: Electric-bed noise stops.

VOICE: Silence.

[pause]

VOICE: S for sound.

SOUND: Cell phone rings. Radio static.

VOICE: Sssssssound.

SOUND: Radio tunes through stations. An ether flutter.

VOICE: But what was it like then?

BROOKES: What was it like then?

SOUND: Faint fluttering.

HISTORIAN: From the beginning of long-distance communications, with fires on mountaintops and so on, we moved to a number of different things throughout history.

SOUND: Flutters move out of reverb.

VOICE: In the siege of Paris . . .

BROOKES: They sent messages by carrier pigeon.

VOICE: On the air . . . waves.

SOUND: Pigeon wings flutter.

BROOKES: What was it like?

VOICE: Can you hear me?

MARCONI: Can you hear anything?

VOICE: Call. Response.

SOUND: Church bell tolling.

HISTORIAN: We get into modern times with Christianity, for instance bells. People were summoned to church by bells. That was the message being sent. And the bells rang over the hills and the dales, and people heard them and answered the call. In fact, John Betchman, I think, called his biography *Summoned by Bells*.

SOUND: Church bell begins digitally "stretching" to a longer timescale.

BROOKES: Before the car, the plane, the radio, the telephone, the telegraph. What was the world like? Was it larger?

BROOKES [in interview]: Did the world feel like a larger place to live in?

SOUND: Church bell continues tolling, now obviously stretched.
CURATOR TWO: I think the world felt enormous. Turn of the century—
and I'm talking about 1800, not 1900—large parts of Africa completely unknown. The Far East, very mysterious. A message to any foreign country took weeks. . . .

That's the beginning of the fifty-minute documentary. Of course, the beginning of a story is just the start of the radio maker's challenge. Keeping a
listener's attention through a long-form documentary means not just delivering information but thinking about story mechanics: how to structure and present that information over the length of the program. There
are a million ways to tell a story, and while creators in other media can
learn from the past (filmmakers or writers can easily go to the library or
the video store to see how Steinbeck, Joyce, Kubrick, and Capra did it), it's
harder for radio makers to study how our wireless predecessors practiced
their art. Who is our Walker Evans, our Hemingway, and how can we hear
them? The Internet is helping to change that, and now we're beginning to
hear some archival radio broadcasts online.

One such recording is a 1936 report on the Moose River mine disaster
in Nova Scotia. It was the world's first live continuous radio remote news
broadcast, and it's not hard to find the audio online. It made a big splash
seven decades ago, broadcast to over 650 stations across Canada and the
United States to an estimated 100 million listeners. The reporter, Frank
Willis, talked into his microphone for three minutes every half hour for
fifty-six hours straight. His presentational style sounds dated to modern
ears, but it was appropriate to the low-sensitivity microphones of the era.
Since there were no tape recorders in 1936 he couldn't rely on recorded
interview clips or field sound. He had only his voice and perhaps a few
hastily scribbled notes, but the poverty of production elements makes it
easier to see the mechanics of what he's doing. He could have arranged his
story in many ways, but here is how he chose to structure this three-
minute report:

Simon McGill . . . is dead.
[pause]
Two others, Doctor D. E. Robertson and Albert Scadding of Toronto,
Ontario, are still in the depths of Moose River mine. Late this after-

noon. They can hang on for eight to ten hours more. But that won't be necessary we don't think. The latest word, sent up though the pipeline which has been sunk into the pit by a diamond drill, brings word from the men below that they can hear tapping. They can hear the men in the workings breaking down the rock to get through to them.

[pause]

It is a broken country down here, drab and desolate. Almost impenetrable from the outside world. You come in over roads almost impassable. A country of scrub and second growth, of rock. Rock, relentless, hard, cruel hard. It is against rock of this sort that miners for the past week have fought and fought, grim-lipped, determined. Every hour, every minute, risking their lives a thousand times an hour, a minute, in a titanic battle to save the lives of two Toronto men. And they are winning their fight. Inch by inch, the rock is retreating.

But another force, sinister and relentless, is creeping up from behind, to possibly snatch a hard-earned victory from these gallant men who have worked so long and so well.

[pause]

We cannot describe to you very well in a few moments the anguish, the mental anguish and the suffering that these men have gone through in the past few . . . or the past week, rather. The past eight days, that's the length of time they've been imprisoned there, but you've followed that all in the press. And it is this water seeping, creeping slowly through a thousand fissures in the crushed and broken walls of the mine, that now sends us the greatest warning. The water is rising.

[pause]

Scant, scarce audible reports from the two surviving men tell us of this menace, creeping ever closer. Making their cramped eight-day tomb even smaller, more cramped, more unbearable. We will not attempt to paint a word-picture of the conditions underground in which these men have miraculously lived for the past eight days. We leave that to your own imagination. The torture of doubt. The calvary of mental and physical anguish. The nerve-destroying sound of dripping water. The rattle and splash of falling rock chips in their prison as another gigantic charge of dynamite is set off to get to them. What must have been the strain, the agony of this past week? You can imagine.

It proved too much for McGill. He lies dead below there. Perhaps mercifully. Perhaps spared from more hours of hoping and listening and praying. But we think not, we believe now that it is possible. But who can say? So many times it has seemed so. So many times things brightened up, looked better, and now . . . who can say?

Here's what I think this long-dead radio maker is doing. In cinematic terms, he opens on a dramatic close-up of a dead man's face. *Simon MacGill is dead.* Okay, did that get our attention? Then he pulls back to a medium shot, revealing two men trapped underground with the body. *Two others . . . are still in the depths.* . . . Next he cuts to a panning long shot of the above-ground landscape. *It is a broken country . . .* and zooms in on all the rock. Now, having shown us the setting, he brings out his dramaturgical tools. This is not just any rock, he tells us, it is *relentless, hard, cruel hard. It is against rock of this sort that miners for the past week have fought and fought.* . . . So now we have protagonist (grim-lipped rescuers) and antagonist (cruel rock) engaged *in a titanic battle.* . . . *And they are winning their fight. Inch by inch, the rock is retreating.*

In other words, slowly but surely the cavalry is coming, and tragedy may be headed off at the pass. Fine, so why should we bother to keep listening? Because the drama becomes suddenly more complex. A third character makes its entrance: *another force, sinister and relentless, is creeping up from behind* . . . and it is the most dangerous of all. Folks, this is a desperate race against time. The villain has tied the fair maiden to the railroad tracks, the hero is too far away, and here comes the locomotive! Can't you hear her pitiful screams? *Scarce audible reports from the two surviving men tell us of this menace.* . . .

Having set up his drama, he fills in some color. *Their cramped eight-day tomb (is becoming) even smaller, more cramped, more unbearable.* In his teasing promise, *We will not attempt to paint a word-picture of the conditions underground,* I hear the old storyteller's schtick of bringing his audience to the edge of their seats and then feigning sudden modesty. I can almost hear his listeners begging, "Oh, please! Please tell us!" and of course he does. Notice how often he urges us to *imagine* the scene? If tape recorders had been invented, no doubt here is where he would have used sound in interesting ways. He uses words instead: *The torture of doubt. The calvary of mental and physical anguish. The nerve-destroying sound of dripping water. The rattle and splash of falling rock chips.* How can they stand it? Will they go crazy undergoing their tortured calvary? Will the rock be rolled away from their eight-day tomb?

At the end, he leads us away from the radio picture which he has painted with a kind of scripted fade. As the scene dissolves he leaves us to ponder metaphysics, extrapolating from this particular mine's drama to larger questions of suffering, surrender, hope, and survival. Death has come to one of the men, *perhaps mercifully. Perhaps spared from more hours of hoping and listening and praying. But we think not, we believe now that it is possible. But who can say?*

Frank Willis was a news reporter who had to communicate facts to the listener, but in order to tell the story he tapped radio's strength as an evocative medium. He was as concerned with drama, story arc, and character as he was with getting the information across to his listeners. These concerns are just as important for effective radio documentary-making in the twenty-first century as they were in Willis's day.

The story arc of my Marconi documentary spans fifty minutes, not three, so it's harder to compress onto the written page. I could suggest that it features a "titanic struggle" between wireless radio (Marconi) and wire telegraph (the transatlantic cable companies) with the water rising on the question of whether the whole story is true or not, but that might be stretching the comparison. My hope is that Marconi himself strides through it less as a carrier of historical information than as a character in a controversial drama. Here's how he first walks onstage:

SOUND: Radio static.

VOICE: Small voice. The still, small voice . . . of the air.

SOUND: Radio static crackle.

VOICE: Can you hear? Can you hear anything?

BROOKES: The place I grew up in: St. John's. The place he came to later.

HISTORIAN: It was a wooden city.

VOICE: What did it sound like?

SOUND [hard cut, on and off]: St. John's harbor ambience, distant hammering, ship's horn.

BROOKES: A city of wood, really. Not like him. He grew up in a city of stone.

VOICE: What did it sound like?

SOUND [hard cut, on and off]: Traffic, voices, bells.

BROOKES: This is what the city of Bologna sounds like today.

SOUND [city sound resumes]

BROOKES: In fact, it's the way it sounds on the Piazza Maggiore, right in the center of Bologna. And near the corner, on 14th November Street, outside Number Seven, there's a stone plaque over the portico that reads, in Italian, "Here was born Guglielmo Marconi, who with electric waves first communicated without cables or wires from one hemisphere to the other, for the benefit of humanity."

VOICE: But what was it like then? What did it sound like then?

SOUND [hard cut]

BROOKES: In 1874.

SOUND: Baby crying, close up.

BROOKES: Introducing our central character. As they would describe him years later in *Vanity Fair* magazine:

FROM *Vanity Fair*: The true inventor labors in an attic, lives chiefly upon buns, sells his watch to obtain materials, and finally after desperate privation succeeds in making a gigantic fortune for other people. Guglielmo Marconi invented in comfort, retained any small articles of jewelry in his possession, and never starved for more than five hours at a time. He is quiet, with a slow deliberate manner of speech, and the shape of his head suggests an unusual brain. He has Irish blood in his veins. His maternal grandfather, Andrew Jameson, of the Jameson whiskey distillery, married a daughter to a Marconi of Bologna, from which union was born Guglielmo. Guglielmo, I may mention, is Italian for "Bill." Being half an Irishman, Bill's lack of more humor is prodigious.

BROOKES: But at this age, his only distinguishing feature is unusually large ears. At least, according to family legend.

VOICE: The story they tell in the family:

BROOKES: Apparently, the family servants were all gathered around Annie Jameson Marconi to have a good gawk at her newborn, and one of the less tactful of them exclaimed:

VOICE: What big ears he has! Hee hee!

BROOKES: Annie replied in a huff:

VOICE: Then he will be able to hear the still, small voice of the air.

SOUND: Radio static clicks on.

BROOKES: And did he hear it?

SCIENTIST: He thought he heard it.

BROOKES: Now why do you say that?

SCIENTIST: Well, from a radio scientist's point of view, he couldn't possibly have heard it. No.

VOICE: There are lots of stories. Is this one true?

SOUND: Radio static clicks off.

There are lots of ways to make radio documentaries. Is this one true?

That Jackie Kennedy Moment

Scott Carrier

MY WORK IN RADIO PRODUCTION can be traced to a moment when I was twenty-one years old, sitting in a college auditorium watching the Richard Leacock film Primary, of the cinéma vérité. I have not seen the film since, so my recollection of what happened is somewhat blurry. In my memory there's a shot about halfway through the film where Jackie Kennedy walks across a hotel room. The lighting is natural, so it's kind of dark, on old black-and-white film. There are maybe ten people in the hotel room, and they are waiting for the results of the Wisconsin primary. Leacock is sitting in a chair with the camera on his lap, and Jackie walks through the frame with a drink in her hand and turns and says something to someone you can't see. You also can't hear what she says, but you can see her smile and maybe she is being coy or maybe she is flirting but she definitely has forgotten that the camera is on. Up till then I'd only seen a stiff woman in still photos, and I'd never understood the public infatuation for her. But in two or three seconds of seeing her act naturally I finally got it—I *saw* Jackie Kennedy. And I thought, I can do that. I can get shots like that and make cinéma vérité films and show the true nature of things.

First I studied documentary film, and then I went to a documentary film school, and then I realized I would never have enough money to make my first documentary film. At that time, 1982, a good 16mm camera and lens cost $40,000, and then there was film and processing and Nagra tape recorders and Steenbeck editing machines. I had ideas, things I wanted to record. I was having Jackie Kennedy moments every day—like watching an old woman in the grocery store or a man cruising down the street in a low rider. The world was happening all around me, and it needed to be recorded or it would be lost, but I could not afford the tools to do it.

So I switched to radio. I already had a tape recorder and a microphone and I'd heard stories on *All Things Considered* by the Kitchen Sisters that made me realize you could do cinéma vérité without a camera. They recorded cultural scenes, like a Bing Crosby golf tournament or a Tupperware convention, and then put the tape together without narration; so the story told itself. Looking back on it now, I was very lucky to hear these stories on the air. I could have easily missed them, and everything would have been different.

For my first story I hitchhiked to Washington, D.C., interviewing the people who gave me rides. I'd hitchhiked quite a bit before that and knew I could get some good tape because people tended to spill their guts if I just sat there and listened. I arrived in Washington with maybe eight or ten good interviews from a wide variety of people, which I thought could be presented as a random cross-section of America—without narration. I was lucky again to walk into the NPR building on a Sunday morning just after the *All Things Considered* people had finished their morning meeting. Lucky because Alex Chadwick was the producer of the show that day, and he was also the producer who'd been playing the Kitchen Sisters' stories. He listened to my tape and he liked it, but then said, "Can you write?" I said I didn't want to write anything, that I wanted to let the people speak for themselves. Alex said that was fine, but nobody was going to listen to the people I interviewed unless I put them in some sort of context, because without context there was no meaning.

"Why did you leave home and travel across the country with a tape recorder and microphone?" he asked.

I said, "Because my marriage fell apart, and I didn't have a job and I couldn't think of anything else to do."

"Fine," he said. "That's the context, that's the story you need to write."

I'm making up these quotes. I can't really remember exactly what we said, but Alex's point was my first lesson in radio production—without context there is no meaning. Reality happens, the events of the world go on around us, but there is no meaning until we provide a context. So I wrote a story to link the interviews together. That's all I thought narration was, a way of presenting the good stuff, the real stuff, the tape.

Strangely, people liked my narration better than the tape. So even though Susan Stamberg said it was the best thing she'd heard on the radio, I felt like I'd screwed up. I'd wanted to make an ethnographic record, but I ended up with a memoir. Not very good cinéma vérité form. I shook it off by deciding to do it right in my next story, which was going to be about a homeless shelter.

When I was working on that first story, I was sleeping at the Gospel Mission at 12th and O streets. I had tape of the guys snoring at night, the dripping sink in the bathroom, a sermon about the prodigal son . . . and a few interviews, the best being with the guy who took me there in the first place—a street singer, a veteran of the Korean War, and an alcoholic. What he said on tape was very good, but you could tell he was drunk. Also black, and poor. So this was a new problem—I had good tape but I couldn't play it.

Luckily, when he sang you couldn't tell he was drunk. In fact, he sang beautifully. It was like you could hear his whole life in his voice. I wrote the story so you never hear him talk but just follow him through an evening and into the next morning, and then at the end he sings a song about Jesus being inside of him. It worked kind of like a cinéma vérité, only I was narrating the part of the camera, which was basically inside my head. And that had to be against the rules.

At that point I decided there were no rules other than to tell the truth. It was wrong to think there was only one way to do it.

When I started working for This American Life, I found I could tell a true story without any actualities at all, just narration, but then, some stories are like that.

Now, when I sit down with all the tape I've recorded while working on a story, I ask myself, "What did I see?" And, "What do I want to show the listener?" I mean, you start on a story thinking one thing is going to happen, and it turns out a bunch of other things happen instead. So what, of all the things that happened, are you are going to present as the "real" thing? For me it helps to have someone ask, "What happened?" And then I pay attention to how I answer the question.

Kerouac said, "Everything I wrote was true because I believed in what I saw." I think that kind of nails it. And then it's important to concentrate on showing rather than telling because when you tell people something they forget it, but when you show it to them, make them imagine it in their own minds, they remember it. This is how it becomes real. So I look for the tape that makes this happen. If I'm lucky, I have a lot of good tape. If I'm not lucky, then I have to write.

IN JANUARY 2006 a Mexican attorney I'd interviewed two years earlier was gunned down on the street in Juarez. His name was Sergio Dante Almaraz, and he was well known in Juarez for speaking out about how the Chihuahuan state government and justice system had been corrupted by the drug cartels.

I went to Juarez in February to learn what happened. I interviewed a friend, a brother, a fellow attorney, and an eyewitness to the crime. I came back with a very interesting story that went nowhere. Everyone I spoke with believed that Sergio had been killed by state police. But no one seemed certain, and all were afraid to say who the police were working for. Sergio himself, two weeks before he was killed, went on a radio talk show and asserted that if he were killed, the assistant attorney general for the State of Chihuahua would be responsible. But after he was killed, of course, the investigation of the murder fell to the assistant attorney general for the State of Chihuahua. She declined to comment, as did her boss in Chihuahua City. They promised an investigation, but I was certain this was a lie.

Writer Charles Bowden, perhaps the leading expert on the world of the border, says it goes like this: First, there is a crime. Say somebody gets murdered. Then there are all kinds explanations for why the person was killed and who was involved for reasons of revenge or not paying a debt, or it was a mistake or a suicide, or witches. Then the stories stop, and it's forgotten. The thing never happened.

This last stage, the thing never happening, is what I was looking at when I came home and started trying to put the story together. All I could say for sure was that Sergio was killed by ten 9mm bullets that went into his head, neck, and chest. Everything else, including the eyewitness account, was questionable. NPR would never play a story about a murder where the only solid fact was a dead body, and yet I owed it to Sergio to do a story about him. The night I met him in 2003, there had been an unspoken agreement between us: he will talk to me, tell me everything he knows; but if he gets killed for speaking the truth, then I will do a story about it. I would not let him be forgotten.

I started trying to put the story together in the spring. Time passed. I couldn't figure out how to do it. People get murdered every day along the border. Why should an American audience care about a dead Mexican they have never heard of? The voices from the tape kept coming up in my dreams, awake and asleep, through the summer, fall, and winter.

I had tape of an interview in an upscale restaurant in Juarez with a friend of Sergio's. He's about sixty years old, a calm and polite man, the host of the local radio talk show where Sergio had announced that he would be killed. We're sitting at the table, and there are plants hanging in macramé, silverware wrapped in white cotton napkins, glasses full of ice water, and he's telling me how years ago he'd been driving down the street with his wife, his mother, and his daughter when a car pulled alongside them and guns went off and he was the only one who lived. He is calm while he is telling me this story. He is calm in my mind as he sits in his car looking at his dead and bloody family. He is calm because he knows his life is over. He no longer feels any pain.

I ask him, "How did you first meet Sergio?" He says he met him thirty years ago, back when they were both living in Mexico City and Sergio was putting himself through law school as a professional wrestler in the Lucha Libre.

These are both good stories, but what do I do with them?

I also had an interview with Sergio's brother, hours of it, in which he lays out a conspiracy theory like a spider's web, a matrix involving his own disappeared son (for two years), a Catholic priest, two drug lords, the old governor, the new governor, the prosecuting attorney, and his mistress. He tells me Sergio came to him two weeks before he was killed and asked him to take care of his two small children.

"So I asked him, 'Why don't you leave, get out while you still can?' and he says to me, 'I am a lawyer. I practice law in the State of Chihuahua, Mexico. This is who I am, so don't ask me that question again.' "

I ask the brother if it's true that Sergio was a professional wrestler when he was in law school, and he says, "Yes, he was Sergio el Hermoso, Sergio the Beautiful."

And then there was the afternoon Julian Cardona and I went to the scene of the crime, an intersection just off Benito Juarez Avenue, a few hundred yards from the bridge to the United States. Julian, an independent photojournalist with a reputation for being incorruptible, was the reason Sergio talked to me in the first place. They'd known each other from back when Julian was working for El Diario, the daily newspaper, before he quit.

In Juarez and other places in Mexico, the media is owned by the drug cartels, so editors and reporters and photographers end up surviving by the things they don't say or report. They get paid for not telling the truth, just as the police get paid for killing people and judges get paid for letting people out of jail. Julian solved this problem by deciding not to get paid. He lives like a monk in a barrio of drug addicts who break into his home on a regular basis even though they know there's nothing inside worth taking. He carries his cameras, two Leicas, with him wherever he goes and keeps his negatives with relatives in El Paso, across the border. If you ask him what's on those negatives he will tell you he has one job—to document the effects of power.

Julian and I are standing in the street where Sergio was killed. The sun is going down, and there are old, torn Lucha Libre posters glued to the walls of the buildings. A block away, a Mexican love song is coming out of a speaker on Benito Juarez Avenue. Julian is explaining that this is a part of town where prostitutes and heroin addicts come to shoot up. He says there are many killings here. I ask him if he thinks Sergio was killed because of the things he told us two years ago, and he doesn't answer the question. So I ask him if he has any hope that the killers will be arrested and put on trial, and he says, "No hope."

"None?" I ask.

"None," he says.

"So what's it like to live in a place like this?"

"Everyday life is like opening the newspapers and finding a new execution, a new. . . . Different faces, same story—killings, rapes, disappearances. Everyday life here. . . . I think no human being can have a sustainable way of life. Like many of my friends, like most of the people I know, they live in the U.S."

"They got out."

"Yes, they got out. So in the past when somebody was telling me, 'We are going to the U.S.,' I didn't understand. But now I understand that it's not easy to live here under this situation, being afraid every day."

"But you stay here, you don't move."

"Yes, because I'm wrong."

This is what he says, but I know it's not what he really thinks. He stays for the same reason Sergio stayed—to fight the bad guy, to battle the forces of evil, to use his camera as a weapon.

These things stuck in my mind, they haunted me, for ten months. Then January 2007 rolled around, and I knew I had to put something together because the anniversary of Sergio's death would be the best and only shot I had at getting a story on the air. So I started over. I asked myself, "What happened? What did I see that I want to show the listener?"

The image that kept coming up was the torn wrestling posters on the buildings at the scene of the crime. I'd taken a photo of them, but what was in my head was not in the photo. What was in my head was the music I'd recorded from a speaker half a block away on Benito Juarez Avenue. A love song, in Spanish, that I don't understand, but when I listened back to it I thought I knew the words:

> The thing of beauty is gone,
> the crying is over,
> the thing of beauty is gone,
> now I can only sing about it.

I thought, that's so romantic, coming from a place swimming in prostitution, drugs, and death. The romantic notion—that love is the strongest force, the first and last force—is so strong once you cross the border. It's so romantic to believe that one man can stand up and fight corruption. In the United States we know about this only from Hollywood movies. Here it's become a myth, but once you cross the bridge into Juarez you can feel it in the air. So I threw out all my tape except for the song and started from there. This is how it came out.

[love song, with traffic in background]
He was sitting in his car, behind the wheel, at a stoplight a block off Benito Juarez Avenue. Four o'clock in the afternoon, long shadows growing down the street. On one side of the street there's a pharmacy, on the other is an abandoned building used by heroin addicts as a shooting gallery. Along the wall of this building there are torn and faded posters of men in masks and capes, ads for the Lucha Libre, Mexican professional wrestling. I wonder if he sat here, wait-

ing for the light to change, looking at the posters, or maybe the posters were why he drove this way to pick up his wife after work. Maybe he came this way to remember when he was young, in Mexico City, going to law school by day and battling the forces of evil by night as Sergio el Hermoso, Sergio the Beautiful.

He knew he was going to die. He'd told his older brother his days were numbered and asked him to take care of his two small children. His brother asked him, "Why don't you leave, cross over while you still can?" And Sergio told him, "I am a lawyer. I practice law in the State of Chihuahua, Mexico. This is who I am, so don't ask me that question again."
[car going by, music continues]
I met him once for an interview, late at night, in his office near the jail. That was three years ago. At that time he was defending a bus driver who had confessed to raping and killing eight young women and burying their dismembered bodies in a vacant field by the factories. In the beginning of the case there had been two bus drivers who had confessed to these crimes, and in the beginning Sergio had a law partner. Sergio and his partner brought the bus drivers into court and showed the judge where they had been beaten and tortured. They showed dried blood on the legs, bruises around the groin where the electrodes had been attached, four inches of intestine hanging out of an anus. The judge responded by saying there wasn't enough light in the courtroom to see.

Sergio and his partner believed the district attorney and the governor of the State of Chihuahua were scapegoating the bus drivers in order to protect the real killers, who they believed were members of the Juarez cartel. They made these beliefs known in public— by speaking to the press and to anyone who would listen. Not long after that, Sergio's partner was gunned down by state police in a car chase through downtown Juarez. The police said they thought he was somebody else. Then one of the bus drivers died in jail under mysterious circumstances. Sergio was threatened, told he would be killed in the same way as his partner.

In 2004 there were state elections, and Chihuahua got a new governor and district attorney. Also, the remaining bus driver was found innocent and released from jail. Victories for Sergio, but he didn't shut up, because nothing had really changed. The justice system was still corrupt.

[car going by]

The car pulled up along side Sergio on the wrong side of the road, to his left, blocking his view of the wrestling posters. I wonder if he knew the man pointing the 9mm automatic pistol at him. I wonder if he spoke before ten bullets flew into his head, neck, and chest. I wonder if he said, My name is Sergio Dante Almaraz, and I practice law in the State of Chihuahua, Mexico.

[music fades up and then out, end]

So what does Sergio Almaraz have to do with Jackie Kennedy? What, after all this, is my point? I started out being blown away by that one short shot of documentary footage because I thought it showed me something real. I've learned since then that reality is always grounded in a story, which is something you and I make up. For me, in the end, there's only one rule: to tell a story that's true.

Talking to Strangers

The Kitchen Sisters (Davia Nelson & Nikki Silva)

Radio to me is a living thing.—SAM PHILLIPS, founder, Memphis Recording Service, Sun Studios, WHER

I still can't put my finger on it. What exactly it is about sound, about sound coming out of a radio that captures me. But whatever it is, it does. I saw a quote from Marcello Mastroianni about why he loved working in the theater, about his "devotion to an art form that evaporates." That gets at some of what I find so mysterious and compelling about radio. I also feel radio is like food. You spend hours, days, months gathering the ingredients, cutting, and mixing—making it cook. The minute it hits the air/table, it's gone—transformed by being eaten, by being heard. Hopefully it was good, and the memory of it lingers. Hopefully, like a good meal, it gathered people together in some way—opened up the senses, sparked emotion and conversation.—DAVIA NELSON

I think telling "story" is what propels me the most—through sound, exhibits, writing, film—I love to listen to good tellers put the words together. Although we don't narrate our stories in the traditional sense, in my mind, Kitchen Sisters' pieces are highly narrated, even though our voices are rarely heard.

I just listened to an air check from 1980 of a Kitchen Sisters' show on KUSP-FM. It was like watching home movies. There we were, pitching during the annual pledge drive, playing snippets of some of our early stories: "The Road Ranger," "Miss California," "Les & Stevie Liebenberg: Trainers and Tamers of Wild Rattlesnakes." We used to do a live two-hour show each week that became the test tube for our early produced pieces. This weekly show contained the kernels of what would twenty years later reconfigure and become Lost & Found Sound. We had never heard of National Public Radio before— no one in our region aired it in those early days, and no one around us was doing produced pieces. I honestly thought we were inventing "the mix."—NIKKI SILVA

SOMEONE AT THE STATION taught us how to use a razor blade, and we began to edit furiously. Whittling, honing little snippets of tape labeled with grease pencil, taped to the walls all around us. We began to work in a method that we have continued to refine over two decades. Sure, now it's digital, but this too will pass. Our techniques seem to endure.

We do extremely long interviews—our average is two hours, but we've been known to go up to sixteen hours over the course of days or months. These epic conversations are contemplated, then cut, recut, distilled to their essence. We can't bear to leave out a particular phrase, a tangent, a moment that made us laugh. The pieces become highly composed—writing with other peoples' words. We are committed to never altering the spirit or intent of what someone says, but we do cut the hell out of them.

Only Connect

Along with this reputation for no narration, which we think of as a sort of ventriloquism—we speak through other people and other people speak through us—what makes our work a bit different is collaboration. There are two of us. Two opinions, two minds and spirits and hearts, two approaches to storytelling, two sets of ethics, two senses of humor. Two people to worry about getting lost on the way to the interview, being on time, remembering to charge the battery.

At first we thought we were unique in this regard, producing nearly all our radio work in collaboration. But we just made it official, gave it a name. The Kitchen Sisters. A radio identity that made it more fun and was mysterious and was easier to pronounce than Davia Nelson and Nikki Silva. But when we look around the public radio landscape, stealth and not-so-stealth collaborations lurk everywhere.

Jay Allison is probably the King of Collaboration, and the list goes on. David Isay with Lloyd Newman and LeAlan Jones, Henry Sapoznik, and now everyone who enters a StoryCorps booth. Ira Glass and every writer in America. Ira and They Might Be Giants. Sarah Vowell, David Sedaris. . . . Mary Beth Kirchner and Nick Spitzer. Or the Hearing Voices Rat Pack, Barrett Golding, Larry Massett, and Scott Carrier (whose windswept voice and stories always make us ache). You get our point. There's a lot to be said for not doing this work entirely alone.

Because as inspiring and educational and challenging as producing radio documentaries is, it can get long and lonesome driving in the middle of nowhere to an interview, listening back to tape that only you will hear until it's all cut and produced and on the air, knowing you couldn't figure out how to keep the best line of the whole interview in, and that now no one will ever know about it but you. Or being holed up editing and mixing for days on end. Or writing grants by yourself. Let's face it, the money sucks; you're not in this work for money (though you deserve it). So you might as well get the deepest, most imaginative, and compelling parts. And have someone to rail about it with and celebrate it with.

The idea behind our work—Hidden Kitchens, Lost & Found Sound, and The Sonic Memorial Project—is just that. Collaboration on a grand scale. Deep storytelling from a variety of perspectives, in a variety of styles and formats—working with hundreds of other people the way we work with each other. An experiment.

We always have six or seven stories in progress at any given time because compelling people or events come along and we have to chronicle or interview or document them even if we're on deadline. It's like we've failed in our "mission" if we don't capture it on tape and present it to a larger audience. The act of bearing witness with a tape recorder is something that feels essential to us and motivates us to move in a lot of directions at once.

Our stories come from the heart and meander down the side roads. We try to entertain each other, make each other marvel and laugh—the odd clipping from an unlikely source, a shard of overheard conversation, stories and gossip from our daily lives. If one can intrigue the other, it's probably what we want to pursue.

We argue a lot. We fret and agonize a lot. We get frustrated a lot. When we're working we each get attached to certain things—a moment, a story, a sound, a "cut this out over my dead body!" sort of thing. Luckily, we mostly agree—on the sound, the shape, and the overall story of the piece. We hear things in the same way. Similar things touch us. We trust each other, and we each care deeply about what the other person thinks. And it's not just the two of us. Behind every Kitchen Sisters story is our great friend and collaborator, sound designer and engineer Jim McKee. He has the secret sauce that makes our work sound that much more distinct, and he is the final arbiter when we just can't agree and need to decide because the piece is due to air in ten minutes.

Oral Mysteries

Another indispensable partnership is the one that forms between the two of us and the person we sit down to interview. We take an oral history approach to interviewing, which isn't always the most efficient way to go time-wise. In an ideal Kitchen Sisters radio world we would interview someone for hours on end, on a specific topic for a specific story, but also have time to go down other paths as they emerge during the interview to get a feel for the larger life of the person. In this ideal world someone else would have come along thirty years before us with a tape recorder and done the exact same thing with this fascinating person, so we could also have that tape to work with and incorporate into the storytelling.

Some of our best stories come to us because we talk to manicurists, butchers, the guy at the other table in the restaurant. We listen to their stories, or tell them ours, and next thing you know, poof, inspiration. Most people are sitting on at least one amazing tale.

When we interview together, one of us is dealing with the recorder, the other has the microphone—and is very close to the interviewee, as close as can be. We try to laugh silently, nod instead of say yes, never say mm-hmm, so we're not stepping on their stories. We maintain eye contact and speak more through facial expressions. Our faces ache when we leave an inter-view. We ask a ton of questions. Sometimes we get on their nerves, we ask so many questions.

We don't turn off the microphone until we're out the door. As soon as the machine is off folks relax and invariably say the line that would work perfectly to start or end the piece. Or they reveal a secret or tell the best joke. When it's time to wrap up we lower our mics but don't turn off the machine. When they start talking again, which they always do, we just casually raise the mic and continue. They're aware we're still recording; we never secretly tape or walk in recording before the person knows we've started.

Life is short. Tape is cheap. Really compelling radio doesn't usually come from tiny slivers of sound. It comes because people got comfortable and spilled the beans or told a long, involved story. Good radio often takes more time than you think it should. We ask people to sing, let them laugh, and we sit quietly through their pauses. You never know.

"Somewhere in the World a Tupperware Party Is Held Every Ten Seconds"

We produced our "Tupperware" story around 1979. It was the second or third piece we had ever mixed. It's a piece that's a result of mistakes—but creating that mix was like a lightbulb going off in terms of our production style. It defined everything that's come from us since.

Here's what happened. It was during the days of the women's movement. You just didn't get invited to a Tupperware party very often. A friend of ours was having one, and we came, with our newly purchased Sony TCD5M cassette recorder. Looking back, here's what we did to get what you hear in the story: (1) recorded the general background hubbub of the party—some of this was distant, some closer (you could make out conversations); (2) close-miked the Tupperware lady as she gave her demo, positioning ourselves next to her; (3) close-miked the guests as they played the Tupperware party games (i.e., going from person to person as they introduced themselves—"I'm Lucky Laurel, and I'll be your Tupperware dealer tonight. . . . She's Lucky Laurel, and I'm Looney Lisa. . . ."). Having close-ups was important because they would grab the listener's ear, giving them a focus within the chaos of the audio party we wanted to create in the piece. Then we interviewed the dealer (who was retiring that night, sick of hauling Tupperware around) and all the guests about the role of Tupperware in their lives.

After that first party we wanted more, so *we* threw a Tupperware party. We also went to a Tupperware sales rally where we recorded the ambience of the room and the rally itself—the singing, speeches, testimonials (if it had been possible we would have plugged into the PA system)—and after the rally, when people were chatting, we did close-miked interviews with everyone we could grab.

The resulting piece is a total construction, layer upon layer of sound, crowded and crammed like a Tupperware party itself. Picture us in the studio with four reel-to-reel machines playing simultaneously (this is long before digital editing) with the levels rising and falling as key words and phrases come and go. The climax of the piece, the Tupperware medley section where dealers recite all of the "benefits" they receive from Tupperware, was a complete accident. While mixing the piece we had several reels of tape going at once, all turned up to equal volume. It was a cacophony of women's voices, but phrases emerged one after another:

WOMAN 1: The gifts that you earn. The last contest that we had, I earned an American Martinsville sofa . . .

WOMAN 2: I've earned an organ, a microwave.

WOMAN 3: I've won a trip, I've gotten a brass bed.

WOMAN 4: I guess you know, Tupperware gives us cars, too . . .

WOMAN 1: I've won a $900 set of Noritake china . . .

WOMAN 5: . . . diamond ring from Tupperware . . .

WOMAN 1: Crystal dinner bells, jewelry boxes . . .

WOMAN 4: My station wagon, I have a brand new station wagon.

WOMAN 1: . . . just little feminine things that women love.

We looked at each other—and that was it. The clutter of plastic bowls, the crowded living room parties, the packed sales rallies. The sound of the piece captured the feeling we were trying to portray in the narrative. Our experiments and our accidents became the sound we were looking for.

Building Community through Storytelling

Our piece "WHER: 1000 Beautiful Watts" is one of the most compelling storytelling and community building experiences we've had. Davia was doing casting work on Francis Ford Coppola's film *The Rainmaker* in Memphis. On the set she met legendary record producer Sam Phillips and his wife, Becky. Sam created Sun Studios and discovered Elvis Presley, Roy Orbison, Howlin' Wolf, Johnny Cash, and Jerry Lee Lewis. In the early days, before he hit it big, Sam supported himself with his Memphis Recording Service. His motto: "We Record Anything, Anywhere, Anytime." He'd record your wedding or funeral or bar mitzvah, beauty pageant or whatever. Sam was a guy with a tape recorder trying to make enough money to support his true passion—to record the music of poor black people and poor white people that he was hearing all around him, that he heard growing up in rural Alabama. And he had always wanted a radio station. (He admired his wife's voice; they had met on the radio in Alabama.) When Sam sold Elvis's contract to Colonel Tom Parker, he used the money to create the first all-girl radio station in the nation, WHER, in the third Holiday Inn ever built. The minute we heard this story we knew we had to chronicle it for our *Lost & Found Sound* series.

We were able track down seventeen of the original WHER girls, as well as the station's console and record library. We produced two twenty-two-minute stories for *All Things Considered* chronicling these women and the life of the station from 1955 to 1971, set against the backdrop of the birth of rock and roll, the civil rights movement, and the women's movement. After the programs aired on NPR, Northwest Airlines flew all the women from Memphis to New York for a tribute to them and Sam at the Museum of Television and Radio in Manhattan. They were in the *New York Times*, the *Washington Post*, *People* magazine. We also had a beautiful WHER reunion for the women and their families onstage at a big national public radio conference in Memphis.

One of the most moving things was hearing from the women's adult children: "Thank you for acknowledging my mother. She never even talked about this. It was never acknowledged that this was an important part of her life as well as historically significant." And this has happened to us with so many of our stories.

DOING A RADIO STORY about some little-known part of history, or a very personal story, can have a significant impact on someone's life, particularly if it's heard by millions of listeners. Somebody out there often has some unfinished business with the story you're telling, something important to add. Our piece "Walkin' Talkin' Bill Hawkins: Searching for My Father's Voice" was about a man who, growing up, never knew his father. His unwed mother could not bring herself to tell him about who the man was. William Allen Taylor became a disc jockey, knowing nothing of the groundbreaking, pioneering work and style of his father, Walkin' Talkin' Bill Hawkins, the first black disc jockey in Cleveland in the 1940s. There were no recordings of Bill Hawkins, and throughout the story the young disc jockey is on a quest for his father's voice, tracking down people from the past—imitating for them what he imagines his father sounded like on the air. The piece aired, and a guy sitting in a rental car listening in Dallas said to himself, "That man is my cousin." Walkin' Talkin' Bill Hawkins had been his uncle. And here was William Allen Taylor looking for his family, looking for the connection. Tony Hawkins contacted NPR, NPR contacted the Kitchen Sisters, and we put the cousins in touch. For the first time, Allen had been acknowledged and accepted into the Hawkins clan. Tony shared dozens of family photographs and helped locate an old recorded air check of Walkin' Talkin' Bill Hawkins. The power of a single story to give someone something that they so fundamentally need astounds us.

A friend of ours teases us and calls it "The Kitchen Sisters Radio Ministry," this deep need to bear witness and try to heal the culture through stories and revelations. But there is truth in what she says. The power of listening, of talking to strangers until they are no longer strangers, of passing on wisdom and humor and knowledge and music, of adding the voices of people whose stories aren't usually part of the national conversation, of creating something haunting and beautiful together, gets us every time.

No Holes Were Drilled in the Heads of Animals in the Making of This Radio Show

Jad Abumrad

I HAVE A GREAT DEAL OF TROUBLE describing *Radio Lab* to people. What I usually say is, well, *Radio Lab* is a series of hour-long radio shows where co-host Robert Krulwich and I wrestle with big ideas (the "eternals" . . . like time, space, consciousness) and mash-up all the usual radio forms. Problem is, that description never inspires shivers of delight. Something about "big ideas" feels like homework. So then I say, okay, well, it's a show about curiosity. And discovery.

Too vague. At this point, the expression of the person I'm talking to flips from boredom to confusion. They then either leave to talk to someone on the other side of the room, or I say, "It makes sense when you hear it."

I believe the job of a great storyteller is to lead people to moments of wonder. But how do you do that?

That's what the ever-persistent editors of this book asked me to address. And so I decided to annotate an actual excerpt from the show. Why tell when you can show, right?

The big question in the following excerpt: Why do we sleep?

(You may think that's a stupid question, but the truth is that no one knows.)

The program starts:

JAD: For centuries people thought that sleep was the opposite of being awake.
ROBERT: Which is reasonable one would think.
JAD: Yeah, because during the day you're doing all these things, you're having all these thoughts and feelings. At night you just lie there.

Very, very still. Like sometimes a bomb could go off, and you wouldn't
wake up.
ROBERT: I can hardly wake up . . . even . . . *long pause* . . . in a fire!
[Robert and Jad laugh like hyenas.]

Not Part of Program: on laughing like hyenas: I know this doesn't look that funny
on paper. But it is, I promise! I only highlight this moment because our show
both fights and depends on these kinds of insane unplanned studio moments. In producing the show, I imagine Improvisation and Composition as
two equally matched boxers (with Bob Krulwich as more of the improviser
and me as the composer). Each show should end in a split decision or else
we've failed. This creates a process that's maybe not the most efficient, but
we do it anyway. First, we outline a segment. Second, we improvise on that
outline, often tossing it out altogether and burning lots of tape that will
never be seen again. Third, we take the best bits of improvisation (the funny
stumbles, the interesting turns of phrase, the places where the beats and
rhythms feel surprising and genuine), and we script around them. After
we've gone through this process two or three times, we usually come out
with a piece of storytelling that's got the right structure and gallop but still
maintains the pleasant illusion of "two guys chatting."

ROBERT: No, I'm a really heavy sleeper. I'm a very, very good sleeper.
JAD: The point is: if all you've got is your eyes to go on. Sleep can seem
   like . . .
ROBERT: Like being off.
JAD: Yeah, like off-ness. Or worse.
[here's a new voice, Carlos Schenck]
SCHENCK: Well, Shakespeare and Cervantes referred to sleep as death.
[musical sting—a mysterious-sounding chord that lingers for a while]

Not Part of Program: on musical sting: We use lots and lots of music. But, as a
guide, I keep the following quote from the great film editor Walter Murch
taped above my desk: "Many film makers use music the way an athlete uses

steroids. No question music can produce strong emotion, but—like steroids—it can also damage the organism in the long run."

As I'm scoring a piece, Walter Murch often gets mad at me (he's become a voice in my head) and reminds me not to "juice" the narrative with emotional information. But the Murch voice sometimes loses to a different voice that tells me that there are times when the music wants to be a character in the story too, with its own point of view (which can sometimes be at odds with the real characters in the story).

But that's not the case here. This sting is used simply as a form of "musical punctuation." It's a big fat comma that separates two thoughts. And because of where it falls, the sting also serves to underline the word *death*.

JAD: That's Dr. Carlos Schenck. He wrote a great book about sleep called *Paradox Lost*.

SCHENCK: We go to bed every night and we die every night. And then we wake up in the morning and we're alive again. That was the prevailing theory for centuries.

JAD: For Dr. Schenck the awakening to just how wrong Shakespeare and Cervantes *were* about sleep came one day while he was sitting in a classroom at school.

SCHENCK: My first year at medical school.

JAD: Back in 1972.

SCHENCK: We had an emeritus professor who was actually a Nobel Prize winner. Dr. Eccles. Sir John Carew Eccles.

JAD: Here's what happened. This esteemed lecturer walks into the class, pops a cassette into the tape deck, hits play . . . and out comes this sound.

SCHENCK: Well, the sound was ptt-ptt-ptt-ptt. Or . . .

[Pause. . . . He taps on the desk with his finger.]

Wait a second. Let me get it right.

[Pause. . . . The sound of shuffling as he searches for something.]

Oh, here we go. . . .

[sound of pen tapping on a metal table]

Take this and multiply by 100.

[Pen taps suddenly whoosh into a blizzard of metallic popcorn snaps and pops that expand into a universe of pink noise drones.]

Not Part of Program: on sound of pen tapping: This is one of my favorite Radio Lab moments ever. Reporter Ann Heppermann interviewed Dr. Schenck and asked him to describe the sound he heard. But instead of asking him to describe the sound as it happened, she asked him describe it as it's happening. She said to him, "Dr. Schenck, rewind in your mind back to the moment you first heard that sound and describe it without using past tense." And remarkably, this simple change in tense flipped him into a different storytelling mode. He was suddenly much more concerned with "getting it just right." So he rummaged around his desk until he found a metal pen and then banged that pen on his metal desk for a few minutes until he produced the right sound. Somehow, Ann forcing him back to the present compelled him to reexperience the moment rather than merely describe it from a distance. That was a real lesson. Bertrand Russell said that the difference between having something told to you and experiencing it yourself is an "unbridgeable gulf." It's that gulf that separates good radio from bad, INMHO.

JAD: This, the professor announced, is the sound of a cat's brain, while asleep.

SCHENCK: My God!

JAD: Schenck almost fell out of his seat.

SCHENCK: This is the brain during sleep? Making these really rapid high-pitched multiple sounds? That just blew us away.

[Metallic popcorn blizzard begins to drift into the ether.]

JAD: Clearly, while that cat was curled up in its little kitty basket, its brain was very, very alive. Much more than anyone expected. And this is still a weird revelation. Like take my cat Sammy.

[My cat Sammy's purring fades in.]

Not Part of Program: on Sammy's purrs: Why insert my motor-mouth cat into a serious piece of journalism?

(A) What's more wonderful and sonically awesome (when recorded on a Shure VP-88 stereo mic and listened to through headphones) than a purring cat?

(B) More to the point, Sammy is an anchoring device. The science of sleep, fascinating as it might be, is still science. And science by its very nature wants to obliterate anecdote and metaphor and personal reflection in favor of pure data. This was an attempt to "concretize" the science.

Ideas are intoxicating, but they're also dangerous. They can quickly drag you away from something that's genuine and real. Like a cat.

JAD: Sammy. This is the sound of my cat Sammy sleeping.

[purrs loudly]

JAD: While Sammy is sitting on my lap, totally out . . . there's a circus happening in his brain.

[quick staccato burst of metallic popcorn]

JAD: What's going on in there?

[back to purring]

JAD: You can imagine that back in the 70s, this was a paradigm shift. People were suddenly like . . .

[cat waking up . . . a meow]

JAD: "Oh my god! If we're gonna find out anything about sleep, we have to ask the brain!"

[here's a new voice, John Lesku]

LESKU: And this is the room where we do all the surgeries.

JAD: And luckily . . .

[door creaking open]

Not Part of Program: on creaking: I'm obsessive about recording the mundane sounds of discovery (the ding of the elevator as we enter a building, walking down the hall, knocking on doors, mic handling noises as one of us fumbles with the recorder) because it reminds the people listening (and us) that this isn't a BBC-style "presentation" in which we're engaged. We're not standing at a podium or across the street from the action and holding our nose—we're right in the thick of it, and we don't know the answers.

JAD: . . . that's easily done, if you're willing to get your hands dirty.

LESKU: So first you've got to make an incision on top of the animal's head. When we've done that, we drill holes through the animal skull.

[drilling sounds]

Not Part of Program: on drilling: We got lots of angry emails about this. Because of the proximity between the sounds of drilling and Sammy's purring, people thought I'd drilled into my cat's head. I didn't, of course. But I can't exactly say that I didn't want them to think I had.

LESKU: And then you insert your electrode.

JAD: Then you've got . . .

LESKU: And that's simply it.

JAD: . . . a little window into their brain. You can see right there on the screen.

ROBERT: Are you out of your mind?! Did you just put a hole into a kitten's head?

JAD: That wasn't my cat! Come on!

ROBERT: What was it that we were doing right there?

JAD: What you heard right there was a mock surgery to an iguana.

ROBERT: Even an iguana. It's not a nice thing to do.

JAD: Look, look, look. The animal was not harmed.

Not Part of Program: on debate: This argument is 67 percent improvised, 33 percent composed.

LESKU: Within twenty minutes of coming out of an anesthetic, the animal is moving around—it's eating, it's climbing, and it's basking. It might seem like a rather invasive procedure, but in actuality, it's not too bad at all.

JAD: And that by the way is John Lesku. He's a graduate student in the ecology department . . .

LESKU: at Indiana State University.

Not Part of Program: on introductions: TV has such an easy time introducing characters because they have the "lower-third" (bottom third of the screen, where they print names and titles). I wish radio had a lower third.

JAD: Which is where we are. John gave our reporter Kara Oehler a tour of the lab.

LESKU: Big boys here. And they all have nice hats.

JAD: He showed her the iguanas.

[here's a new voice, Kara Oehler]

OEHLER: These here are a little frightening to me. They're pretty huge.

JAD: Four feet long, head to toe.

ROBERT: I didn't know that.

JAD: I mean, they look like baby alligators.

LESKU: Pick that one up.

JAD: And John measures their brain waves at night to see what happens in their head while they sleep. In a way it's a continuation of that cat experiment that Dr. Schenck just told us about, except what they're looking for is much more peculiar than could ever happen in a cat. Or in us.

ROBERT: What is that?

JAD: Let me put it to you as a puzzle. Forget iguanas. Think dolphins. All right? Dolphins.

ROBERT: Yup.

JAD: How is it that a dolphin in the ocean, or even the dolphins that you might find at Six Flags in New Jersey. . . .

[splash! sound of dolphins flapping in water, squeaks]

JAD: They have two.

[here's a new voice, Megan Tutera]

TUTERA: Cody is our ten-year-old Atlantic bottlenose dolphin. His buddy Avalon is twelve years old.

Not Part of Program: on dolphins: Another mini-anchoring device, like Sammy. Why talk about dolphins in the abstract when there are real dolphins to be found right across the Hudson River at Six Flags in New Jersey? A small but effective way to force information into experience.

JAD: And that's her trainer, Megan Tutera. Avir Mitra is holding the mic. Anyhow, here's the puzzle. We asked Megan about this. How is it that her two dolphins, Cody and Avalon, can successfully sleep given the inherent challenges of being a dolphin?

ROBERT: I don't . . . what do you mean the challenges of the dolphins?

JAD: Well, they have significant challenges, my friend. First of all, they have to breathe.

TUTERA: They're conscious breathers. They're not unconscious breathers, so they've got to think about breathing.

JAD: Making matters worse, dolphins are not fish, so they have to breathe air. Which means they have to constantly, consciously come up to the surface.

[sound of surfacing dolphin, blows air out of blowhole]

JAD: So you can imagine what would happen if they went unconscious for a while.

[dolphin squeaks]

ROBERT: It would drown.

[more dolphin squeaks, these ones a little demented]

JAD: And yet they do manage to sleep, a lot.

ROBERT: How long?

JAD: Eight hours a day.

ROBERT: Really?

JAD: Like us. Yeah. Eight hours.

ROBERT: But how?

JAD: That's the puzzle.

TUTERA: What happens is that they do what we call logging. It's when they rest on the surface of the water. When a log floats down a river, it just floats. That's exactly what they look like. And they rest half their brain at a time.

[ambient music up]

Not Part of Program: on music: Music for emphasis, for underlining, not for forcing feelings. The music here has the effect of gently exalting the passage that follows. The Murch voice is right, people don't want to be told what to feel . . . but they *do* want to be told what to pay attention to.

[here's a new voice, *Radio Lab* intern Avir Mitra]

MITRA: Half their brain is asleep?

TUTERA: Half their brain is asleep at a time.

JAD: That is nature's solution. To cut the dolphin brain in half.

ROBERT: You mean literally?

JAD: Literally in half. So that one half can snooze while the other half keeps the dolphin swimming and surfacing just enough to breathe. From the outside you can't really tell what's happening. It just looks like the dolphin is sort of awake but a little out of it.

TUTERA: So it's almost like this state of when you're falling asleep but if something happened you'd wake right up. So they're in that state all the time.

[here's a new voice, Steve Lima]

LIMA: It sort of can be characterized as groggy.

JAD: That's Steve Lima. He runs one of the labs back at Indiana.

LIMA: They're sort of awake, and they're sort of asleep. It's just a way of staying awake enough.

JAD: And again, it's easy to miss, but if you look inside that groggy dolphin's brain at what the brainwaves are doing . . .

LIMA: It's exquisitely obvious.

JAD: Clear as day.

LIMA: A six-year-old could figure it out. One-half of the brain has these beautiful slow waves . . .

[smooth, pure tone rises and falls in a gentle sine wave pattern; only heard in the left ear/speaker]

LIMA: . . . like a sine curve. And the other one is just . . .

[jaggedy chaotic sound zigzags frantically; only heard in the right ear/ speaker]

LIMA: Just jagging all over the place.

ROBERT: Wow. That is amazing.

JAD: It's called uni-hemispheric sleep. That's what the guys at Indiana State are really interested in. Because . . . and here's the next surprise. It seems to go way beyond dolphins.

LESKU: Oh, yeah! Yeah, aquatic mammals like whales, seals, and sea lions.

JAD: John says that all the marine mammals seem to do it, too.

LESKU: Recently walruses. They're all found to engage in uni-hemispheric sleep as well.

JAD: And now the Indiana team, led by this guy . . .

[here's a new voice]

AMLANER: I'm Charles Amlaner, chair of the Department of Ecology and Organismal Biology.

JAD: They found this weird split brain behavior in creatures of the air.

ROBERT: Ohhh . . .

It's not just water mammals and birds whose brains are split in two. Humans have two cranial hemispheres. There's the analytical left brain, which wants "explanation." And then there's the free-associative right brain, which wants "experience." (This is a terrible oversimplification, of course, but hey). The point, if you're a storyteller, is simply this: the story you tell should speak to both halves. A good story shows there's magic in experience. And that magic is what keeps butts in seats. (It occurs to me now that maybe the reason we improvise so much, sometimes to the point of crushing inefficiency, is that that's our way of staying connected to the actual "experience" of storytelling). On the other hand, the best stories connect experience to something larger. An idea, a slightly new perspective, a sense of something universal that's shared, human to human. Maybe even human to duck.

Harnessing Luck as an Industrial Product

Ira Glass

I STARTED WORKING AT National Public Radio's headquarters in Washington when I was nineteen, but I wasn't competent at writing and structuring my own stories until I was twenty-seven. I've never met anyone who took longer, and I've met hundreds of people who work in radio. Back then, I made my living by filling in as a production assistant on the various national news shows, and by taking day jobs as a temp typist around Washington. I was sort of hopeless at all the basic tasks of recognizing and shaping a story.

If this sounds like exaggeration, here's a typical report from when I was in my mid-twenties. It opens with sound, hubbub, and Muzak from a grocery store. I begin:

> It's not such a long way from the local grocery store to the international debate over whether sorghum and meat production are causing corn to decline in Latin America.

Oh right. That debate. Which doesn't actually exist.

> There's a general air of prosperity here, partly thanks to Mexican imports of U.S. grains, which help boost our farm economy.

From the choice of words to the sentence structure to the idea at its heart, it would be difficult to write more boringly.

> Mexico is now one of our biggest grain customers, buying a half billion to a billion dollars worth every year, including corn to feed its people and sorghum to feed its livestock. This helps cut our own trade deficit and benefits everyone in the U.S. economy. But in Mexico this policy has led to fewer tortillas for the poor, and unappetizing tortillas for everyone else.

What's sad is that the idea behind this story is actually kind of interesting. If I were to summarize that idea today, I'd say: Because it's so profitable to sell food to the U.S., the best farmers in Mexico export to us instead of feeding other Mexicans. We eat better, and Mexicans eat worse. Cool, right? But the way I wrote this at twenty-six, it's hard to even tell what the story is about. The language is stilted. I throw around terms like "trade deficit" and "imports of U.S. grains," not to mention "general air of prosperity," as if these are phrases people say out loud. It violates one of the basic laws of radio: that you should never say a sentence on the air that you couldn't say in a normal dinner conversation.

What's more, the tone is all wrong. There's no pleasure, no sense of discovery, no humor, no genuine human moment, no fun. And I'm a horrible reader, underlining every other word for emphasis.

A few years ago, one of the producers of This American Life, Alix Spiegel, had an idea for a story about chickens, and I remembered that I'd worked on a similar idea as part of this same supermarket series. I dug up a tape. She listened. "There's nothing in here," she reported to me, "showing any talent at all. There's nothing in here that indicates that you were ever going to get it."

I think for anyone starting off in any kind of creative work, this is the most daunting thing about it, this period when you're lost, not very skilled, and you have no idea if you'll ever get the skills you're hoping for. For some people this period just lasts a year or two. For me, it took eight years.

I did everything I could think of to speed things along. I forced myself to do a lot of stories, put myself in a position where people were expecting work out of me. Sometimes these were paid gigs. Sometimes they were free. And I created little projects for myself. Many of these were designed to sidestep my shortcomings as a writer and reporter. I'd interview people, get them to tell me amazing anecdotes from their lives, and then edit myself out completely. To make the transitions work from one quote to the next, I'd use music.

BY THE TIME I was in my thirties, I was getting reporting assignments from NPR, and on any given story, in addition to whatever my editor wanted, I had my own goals. For instance, every story—even the stories thrown together in one day—had to have a tape-to-tape transition. That is, the story would go from one quote directly to the next . . . or from a quote to location sound to another quote, with no narration. This was to keep me alert to pacing. Too many radio stories get into this rhythm of script then quote then script then quote then script then quote. That's poor craftsmanship. And boring.

Every story also had to have some moment that was there just to amuse me. A funny moment, an emotional moment, some original observation I'd made on the scene that no other reporter had. This could be just one nice line in the script.

Every story had to have someone who was more than a talking head, spouting policy points. Someone had to have human flesh to them, human motivation, a little humor, a real emotion. This sometimes only took a line of description, a thought about who they were and why they believed what they believed, a surprising moment, a funny interaction with me on tape.

Which brings me to my next point. Every story had to have some moment where I was in the tape, talking to someone. I did this because I'd noticed that in other people's stories, the most interesting stuff usually came when they interacted with the people in the stories, where there was a back and forth. It allowed for a different kind of drama in the stories, the drama of someone being charming or dogged or wheedling or funny with another person. This didn't come easily to me. Like most beginning radio reporters, I didn't like to hear myself on tape. I didn't like how I sounded asking the questions. I was awkward. I was cloying. Trying too hard one way or another. It was embarrassing. But at some point I decided that omitting this kind of tape meant I was also eliminating a certain drama from my stories, throwing away one of the most powerful tools at my disposal, and I forced myself through it, in story after story. Slowly, I got better at asking questions on tape. I still think the quickest way beginning radio reporters can make their stories more interesting is to get themselves on tape, asking tough questions, cajoling, joking, really talking to the interviewee.

Another discovery that changed everything was when I realized I could imitate the people I liked on the radio. I know that doesn't sound profound. Or dignified. But people in every other creative medium do it: painters and songwriters and filmmakers. It's part of learning your craft.

The writer David Sedaris has said that when he was starting out he would copy passages from favorite books. "I wanted to sense what it must have been like to write these words for the first time," he declared. "I would type them hesitantly, pretending that they had just come to me." I understand that. In my twenties, I'd sit by the radio with a stopwatch and do rough, real-time transcriptions of entire half-hours of *All Things Considered*. How many sentences does a reporter usually say before his first piece of tape? How many seconds is that? How many sentences are there between pieces of tape? What makes an interesting host intro, and a boring one? How many quotes are there in a three-minute story? And in a four-minute story? NPR reporters usually finish one piece of narration and one piece of tape, which is the basic unit of broadcasting—the setup for the tape and then the tape—every thirty-five to forty-five seconds. (Or at least that's what it was in the 1980s when I did my timing.)

I remember stealing this one move I'd heard Alex Chadwick make in a story. It's become one of the signature moves that I and the other people on my radio show do. It defines the style of our show.

I noticed Alex's use of it in a story about frogs.

A high school girl refused to dissect a frog in class. She thought it was inhumane to kill frogs for the purpose of teaching biology. A judge ruled that she still had to do the assignment, but the school had to provide her with a frog that had died of natural causes. I was working at *All Things Considered* and saw this item in the paper and thought it was pretty funny, that some school administrators were now going to have to find frogs who were just on the verge of dying, or had just recently died, and so I produced a little story with Alex about it. To illustrate the hell this high school science teacher would soon find himself in, we went with a naturalist to a swamp to look for some newly dead or dying frogs.

So, okay, you're Alex Chadwick. You have to write the opening of this story. Most of us would be kind of workaday and boring about it. We'd write something summarizing the court case, maybe along the lines of what I just wrote above:

A few weeks ago in Victorville, California, a high school girl refused to dissect a frog in biology class. Her teacher insisted, and they all ended up in court, where a judge came to this Solomonic ruling: she still had to do the assignment . . . but the school had to provide her with a frog that died . . . of natural causes. But does such a thing even exist? We decided to figure it out.

That's lame, I know, but I'm making a point. I remember when Alex showed me his script, I was stunned at how long the opening was. I figured he'd knock it off in three or four sentences, but he was taking so much time. (And needless to say, because we were on *All Things Considered*, we needed things to be short.) I thought he was nuts. But what he'd done was so much more engaging than what most radio writers do, because it actually had a human voice to it. He sounds like a real guy telling you about something he's interested in, not a news-robot:

> We've delayed a few days bringing you this story because it hasn't had an ending. It still doesn't, but we're going ahead anyway, with our own modest contribution to developments. Here's the situation: In southern California, in Victorville, at Victor Valley High School, Jennifer Graham, age sixteen, would not carry out an assignment in biology class. She refused to dissect a frog. She said that it bothered her that any creature should have to die so that she could cut it open for study. It was a matter of principle. And as with many such issues, it wound up in court.
>
> On Monday, a judge in Los Angeles issued this ruling: Jennifer must study the innards of a real frog rather than the plastic model or computer mock-up she'd proposed. But the school must provide a frog which has died of natural causes. That's right, natural causes.
>
> "Excellent idea," responded a lawyer for the school, perhaps happy with any solution. "If we have to station someone down by the swamp, or wherever it is they live, to see them die, we'll do it." And his partner added, "Frogs don't live very long anyway."
>
> Indeed, how difficult could it be with all the frogs in the world to find one that had naturally . . . croaked.

[KERPLUNK, swamp noises]

CHRISTIE CRAWL: Don't stand in one place too long or you get sort of stuck in the muck.

REPORTER: Ah, yeah, I think I am stuck in the muck.

CHRISTIE CRAWL: Great hiding places for frogs.

REPORTER: A naturalist named Christie Crawl—really!—agreed to help us search for a naturally dead frog at a swampy area she called a "wetland" over at the Huntley Meadows Park in Virginia. We waded out to where the dark water was knee deep. Something squawked gently.

CHRISTIE CRAWL: That was a frog . . .

Pretty nice, huh? So let's back up a little, and I'll show you his big move.

> . . . it bothered her that any creature should have to die so she could cut it open for study. It was a matter of principle. And as with many such issues, it wound up in court.

See that? The stuff about it being a matter of principle, and the phrase "as with many such issues"? He steps out of the facts of this particular story and toward a big general point about How Things Work. I remember hearing that and noticing the feeling it gave the story and wanting my stories to have that feeling. Just imagine the script without Alex's key phrases:

> . . . it bothered her that any creature should have to die so she could cut it open for study. And she wound up in court.

Not as grand, right? Not as knowing. I later noticed that lots of great nonfiction writers—Malcolm Gladwell, Michael Lewis, Susan Orlean, James Fallows, David Foster Wallace—are constantly pointing out the general principles at work in anything they're reporting. Here's Michael Lewis, for instance, writing about a teenager who refused to cooperate with a lame government plan: "That's the trouble with fourteen-year-old boys—from the point of view of the social order. They haven't yet learned the more sophisticated forms of dishonesty."

This eventually became such a big part of my style as a writer, and the style of the radio show I work on now, that opening my script for last week's program, I come to an example of it immediately, in the intro to Act One:

> And now . . . the story of a man with a simple mission: to give a little special treatment to a group of people whose contribution to society is often overlooked, the men and women of the food service industry.

Not the greatest piece of writing but a decent one. Thanks, Alex.

AFTER YEARS OF TRYING, I got to the point where I was reporting stories all the time for NPR's daily news programs, and these stories had scenes and characters and plot twists, funny moments and emotional moments. Some were breaking news. Some were features. NPR sent me into a high school for a year, and I filed a story every couple of weeks about the kids and teachers there, and why it's so hard to change things in a public high school. I also had a few writers I would edit and produce as commentators for Morning Edition and All Things Considered: David Sedaris, Sandra Tsing Loh. I'd mix music under their commentaries, which was rarely done on NPR.

It seemed like someone could make a nice show that combined these emotional, funny, hard-to-turn-off documentary stories and these amazing radio writers. And in 1995, when Chicago Public Radio moved to a new facility and was looking for an innovative show to put in that building, that's the idea I pitched.

Over the years, I'd developed some very strong ideas about the best way to structure a story for radio, and I employed these on the new show, This American Life.

Those ideas are pretty simple. I usually think of a radio story (at least the kind of story we do on This American Life) as having two basic parts to it. There's the plot, where a person has some sort of experience. And then there are moments of reflection, where this person (or another character in the story or the narrator) says something interesting about what's happened.

Put another way, there's the action of a story, and then there are the conclusions.

Both have to be pretty interesting. A person can walk through lava, cure a disease, find true love, lose true love, discover he was adopted, discover he was not adopted, have all manner of amazing experiences, but if he (or the narrator) can't say something big and surprising about what that experience means, if the story doesn't lead to some interesting idea about how the world works, then it doesn't work for radio. Or, anyway, it's not going to be as powerful as the best radio stories. The best radio stories have both. So one way to get an ailing story to work (and to determine if it's a story at all) is to figure out what surprising conclusions about the world might come from that story.

And here's something counterintuitive. It's best to try to figure out the potential Big Ideas in any story before you go out interviewing people. On *This American Life*, we'll talk about these ideas as part of our story-selection process. We won't start a story if we can't imagine the kinds of ideas it'll lead to, the questions it'll answer. We need those at the beginning of the process to help us figure out what tape the reporters will have to get in the field.

SO HOW DO YOU FIND the Big Ideas? Consider this story. It's about a guy, Adam Davidson, whose mom is Israeli and whose dad is American. When he was a teenager, Adam read the biography of David Ben-Gurion, the founder of the state of Israel. Ben-Gurion was a compulsive diarist, and when Adam was sixteen, he decided to keep his own diary, writing each day with the quiet conviction that he, Adam, was destined for a fate like Ben-Gurion's. Someday he would be the prime minister of Israel.

Adam's a regular contributor to our show, and doing the story was mainly an excuse to read his cringe-worthy teenage diary entries on the air. Here's a sample:

ADAM [reading]: January 9, 1987. There's so much wrong with Jews in
    Israel that I'm going to have a job ahead of me. One thing is the lack of
    any strong Jewish identity among most Jews. This attitude sickens me.
    I do not know exactly what I will do, but if this situation continues
    when I'm a bit older, than watch out world Jewry, here comes Adam!
IRA: [incredulous laughter]
ADAM [talking now, not reading]: And "COMES ADAM!" was all in capital
    letters.

Interviews for this style of story (and most interviews I do for our radio show) generally take the following form: For a while I get the person to lay out the plot of what happened, getting them to be very specific about each plot point, about what people said to each other at the pivotal moments, expanding and commenting on any little details that happen to interest and amuse me. In this case that included reading from diary entries. This is usually a chronological rendition of the story. We start at the beginning and go through the whole thing. Sometimes I'll make them tell a key section two or three times if I feel like I don't have it yet. "Wait, wait, wait," I find myself saying. "Just give me that part again so I can be sure it's clear. What did he say to you, and what did you do? Just tell me again."

And then there's the part of the interview—really, it can be interspersed throughout the interview—where I look for the Big Ideas. Once I had Adam explain the diary and read a bunch of funny excerpts, I started fishing around, asking every idea-oriented question I could possibly think of.

To come up with these questions, I imagine the story from Adam's perspective. I try to imagine what it would mean to be that sixteen-year-old version of Adam, and what the story says about kids like that. The questions can be as direct as "Why you? Why were you the one kid who thought he'd be prime minister of Israel?" Or the questions can be abstract, to elicit a more general answer: "What sort of teenager do you think ends up writing a diary like this?"

In the end, out of all the questions I asked, two led to interesting thoughts. One came from the questions about what sort of kid he'd been. Adam said he was awkward, disliked for being a know-it-all at school, never had a girlfriend, and so it was nice when he was sixteen to have this alternate life in his diary, as a future world leader.

ADAM: I didn't have much angst about being the future prime minister of Israel. I was very calm and confident and comfortable with it. And I had so much angst about every other aspect of my life, and so I now see it as, maybe it was a good solution, you know? It was a good way to deal with what I was going through to have this space where I could just be, you know, one of the greats. I'm not just a sixteen-year-old kid who, you know, is having crushes and, you know, a hopeless geek who can't get a girl to kiss him, being scared and confused about growing old. I'm the future prime minister of Israel, and everything goes through that.

But the really beautiful and original and surprising part of the interview came by accident, out of a question that was actually a throwaway.

IRA: And Adam, what would the sixteen-year-old think of you now?
ADAM: I think he'd be really disappointed. I think he'd be really sad.

I didn't expect this at all, and when he said it, I knew we were onto something good. So I stayed with it.

IRA: Because you're not the prime minister of Israel?

ADAM: Yeah, because I just have such a small life. I mean, I remember I
was really disappointed and really sad about my parents. I mean, I was
reading biographies, of course, about all the prime ministers in Israel.
And I would just think about my parents and think, how do you wake
up every day knowing that your actions won't affect millions of people? Like, how is that enough motivation? You know, just to have your
petty little craft and your petty little family and your small little apartment, you know. It just seemed pathetic.

[pause]

At this point I've gotten to that place that's so hard to get to in any radio
interview. He's talking completely from the heart. He's talking about himself, but he's also describing something universal. Honestly, if you've never
felt that feeling, that way of looking at your parents, then you were not a
teenager in America. It's so big and easy to relate to. This is the kind of tape I
live for. But Adam continued:

And they have the kind of life, you know, that basically, I want for
myself. Just to have a craft that I enjoy and make a living at and have
a family.

He's working out an idea that's in his head, in real time, out loud. Trying
to make sense of something that touches him deeply.

When I get to this rarified place with an interviewee, I do everything
possible to try to stay there. I try to keep the trance going. I ask as many
follow-up questions as I can think of, spelling out all the implications of
what's being said.

IRA: What you're saying, though, is that the sixteen-year-old you would
be cringing at the thirty-year-old you just as the thirty-year-old version is cringing at the sixteen-year-old.

ADAM: Yeah, that's very true. Yeah. He would be very, very disgusted if
he heard this radio piece.

IRA: And embarrassed.

ADAM: And embarrassed. He'd be really embarrassed. It would seem like
I had settled. In a pathetic way.

This sequence takes a small, funny story and makes it special. But to get that nice answer on tape—to get so lucky—I had to try dozens of different things during the interview. I threw out all sorts of half-baked questions, speculations, and proddings. To give you a sense of just how far-ranging and ill-conceived some of these were, here's a transcription of some of the Big Idea questions that went nowhere in that one-hour interview.

Although it's hard to resist the temptation, in the interests of honesty and pedagogy, I am not cleaning up my often dreadful syntax and word choices.

> I wonder how old you were when you crossed over to when, if you read the diary, you would cringe after it? Do you think like two years after you wrote it? Four years? Six years?

> Do you think you're doing things now that you'll cringe at sixteen years from now?

There are lots of questions about cringing in this interview, because it was done for a show we were putting together about "cringes" (though, as often happens, it eventually ended up in a completely different episode).

> Well, the thing that makes the diary cringe-worthy is that the sixteen-year-old you so aggressively believes certain things that seem so wrong-headed to you now, and I'm wondering do you even believe things as aggressively as this sixteen-year-old now? Do you believe in anything this aggressively?

> Do you still believe that you have a destiny that you are supposed to fulfill, and that you could fail at it?

> I wonder if seeing who has ended up as the prime minister—as you and I record this it's Ariel Sharon—gives you any sort of comfort in the fact that maybe it's not the most exalted job in the world?

IRA: Now, we should point out that you weren't in Israel at all.

ADAM: During the writing of this diary I wasn't in Israel at all. It reminds me of the fact that many historians believe that much of the Bible was written in Babylonian exile hundreds of years after the events that they mention, you know, King David or the Exodus of Egypt, and the Bible was infused with passion specifically because no one who wrote it had any access to the stuff they were writing about.

IRA: Wait, what does that have to do with the diary?

ADAM: Just that this diary was written by a kid outside of Israel.

IRA: Oh, I see, much like the Jewish people when they wrote the Bible under this theory, in exile, away from the Holy Land. You, yourself, were exiled from the Holy Land.

ADAM: In exile from the Holy Land, away from the nation that I would some day serve and lead.

IRA: You were in New York City, and so you were creating your document.

ADAM: Exactly, yeah.

IRA: Your Torah, if I will.

ADAM: [laughs] Right. This is the Torah of Adam Davidson.

So many of the things I said to Adam are embarrassing to see here in print. But this is typical for me. I don't want to sound dumb on the air, but I'm willing to sound dumb during an interview. And trying lots of different ideas, including dumb ones, is the only way I know to get the kind of tape I want.

And yes, lots of times I discover that either no one in the story has anything interesting to say about what happened, or the facts of the story turn out differently than I thought, or some other damn thing fails to fall into place and the story just dissipates into vapor. Half the interviews I do never make it onto the air for this very reason. Our radio show's budget is built around the premise that we'll kill (and pay for) a third of everything we start.

But I've made peace with the idea that doing this kind of work always amounts to going out in the world, poking around, trying one thing after another and waiting for luck to strike. If you want to get hit by lightning, you have to wander around in the rain for a while.

It's funny that when you decide you want to do creative work—journalism or music or films or whatever—nobody tells you how much of your time you'll be spending simply hunting for something worth writing about. I remember when I was young, looking around at all the other reporters, it seemed like they all had a million ideas, without even trying. I wondered what was wrong with me. I didn't realize that searching around for stories was a big part of the job, and if I spent half my time doing that, I was doing as well as anybody else.

Nobody tells you to amuse yourself either. Now that I'm here in the next-to-last paragraph of this essay, the thought occurs to me that that's one of the biggest things I learned along the way too. That the easiest way to make something that other people will love is to be out for my own fun.

So that's how I see my job now: To try a thousand things until something interesting happens. To push on the half-baked ideas and stories as hard as they can be pushed. And to follow my curiosity. To keep trying different things until luck kicks in. Luck will always kick in.

Covering Home

Katie Davis

Washington, D.C., January 1995

I HOLD MY MICROPHONE in my lap as the cop turns up Fifteenth Street.
"Lots of guns where I'm taking you." I know he's not bragging. The year
has barely started, and D.C. is counting up shootings—on the streets and
in schools.

The cop picks up Columbia Road, near my home. *Don't know this way.*
Every morning I take the bus downtown, my pocket radio piping the
morning news into my earplugs until I reach National Public Radio. I get
to work two hours early to read the *New York Times*, the *Washington Post*, and
the *Philadelphia Inquirer*. Clip, pitch, book interviews. Cut tape, write, and
put the story on the air. That's my job and all I want is more hours in the
day to do it.

"Gonna check behind Fuller," says the cop. I am always thinking about
the big international stories like South Africa. Just days before, I asked the
foreign editor to send me there to do a follow-up to an earlier trip in the
mid-1980s when I was sent to produce stories on the fight against apartheid. I spent time in Alexandra Township as the young people made their
stand in the rocky fields. They danced their fury, sang their change. The
soldiers faced them with rifles; the young people picked up the rocks at
their feet. This was the story I knew; the names of the underground leaders, the details of their strategy to make the black townships impossible to
govern. I knew almost nothing about the city I had grown up in, the
young people who were my neighbors.

The cop cuts his lights and coasts into an icy alley. "I'm going in here." I
roll tape. "There, down by the end," the cop nods. A figure is hunched
inside a puffy coat. "See the way that guy is weighted down on the left?
Could mean a gun in his pocket." Last year, 121 handguns were confiscated
in this neighborhood. The cop clicks his radio, tells the dispatcher, "I'm

doing a stop." We wait, until headlights bloom and the back-up cruiser pulls into the other side of the alley. The figure stiffens as he is surrounded.

"I'm gonna check in your pockets," the cop half asks, half warns, "hands up," and the cop pulls out two metal padlocks on a chain from his jeans. "Protection officer, protection," says the boy, no older than fifteen. "We need it out here." "Go home," says the cop. No gun, but he confiscates the homemade weapon. "It's sixteen degrees out here."

As we leave the alley, we turn left, then right. *Don't know this way either.* Across a wide avenue, and we're on Columbia Road, *my Columbia Road.* The city's gun problem is here in the neighborhood I grew up in. I have statistics from the police and the FBI—numbers and no explanations. This is my childhood neighborhood, and I cannot explain why a boy carries a weapon. *Who is his enemy?* The whys of South Africa, these I know. I want to shelve this story, move on, but I write it and put it on the air. I do not fully understand my misgivings at this point. I only know that after fifteen years of reporting and producing for NPR, this is the first time I feel like a fraud. *I did not speak to one young person for this story. I do not know how they feel out on the streets, why they might want a weapon.*

By that spring, I leave National Public Radio—over an unrelated matter, a pay-equity dispute. I have never worked anyplace else—never wanted to—and I am unmoored. I am not sure about my future or whether I even want to work in journalism anymore. For months, I do little except walk my dogs around the neighborhood and sit on the front porch of the house I grew up in. And it is in this sitting that I begin to listen to my neighbors and reshape how I hear and tell stories—closer to home.

A boy rumbles by on his skateboard, says his name is Julio and asks to pet the dogs. *Sure.* Another twelve-year-old bellows like a carnival hawker, "Hey lady, you got a tire patch?" *Sure.* And I give Joaquin ten dollars to run to the bike store to buy three patch kits, one for him, and the rest I'll keep for other kids. The super from the building down the street notices the cluster of kids and lugs up two old bikes he found in the alley. And this is how, without planning, I start a recycle-a-bicycle program on my front porch. Everything takes place on my front porch for a long while.

I become known as the "bike lady," the lady who always has granola bars and time to sit and listen. After a year, I form a youth group called the

Urban Rangers and begin raising money to pay for bike parts and snacks. Two teenagers ask me to start a basketball team. *Sure, why not?* And then I explain my philosophy to the guys, that winning is not important on this team, and everybody will get to play in every game. "No, no," the boys interrupt and begin coaching me on how to be a coach. The dialogue is funny and that night the rusty part of my radio brain begins chanting, *Good tape. Good tape.*

So, I call an old friend at NPR and float the idea of writing an "essay with tape" about my team. I warn the show producer that the story will be personal, like a diary, that I break the rules of journalism in every paragraph. I write in the first person, and I have not kept any objective distance from these boys. I give money to two brothers because I know they are hungry. I hire another kid's father because they are struggling on $12,000 a year. The boys hang out at my house, they come to tell me about problems. I no longer wanted any distance between me and these neighborhood kids. NPR solves the issue of my status by calling me a commentator. My transition from reporter to commentator took four years of neighborhood porch sitting and trouble shooting and is distilled into this one word.

"*Diary of a Wannabe Basketball Coach*"
By midseason, we're losing every week. One team, South East, blows us off the court playing so smoothly, it looks choreographed. They have what the kids call "hops and handles." They can jump and dribble brilliantly. And they hopped and handled us right up and down the court to the tune of 105 to 70.

ANDRE: You the main one be complaining! Moping.

There's raw emotion when we lose; glares, pouting, finger point-ing. Hugs do not work at this point. The hardest thing, though, is that every time we lose, the postgame talk settles on one point—the referees. It's a mantra for the kids: "The referees cheated, we lost because the refs cheated." Here are Wiley and Clayton.

WILEY: He wasn't calling nothing. He was calling everything against us. The other team was just collecting their points. He was straight cheating.

KATIE: Do you really think a ref would cheat?

CLAYTON: Yeah, if they paid them. Anyone can pay a coach. That's how we lost in football.

And so it goes. My response is to keep saying, The minute you think about a call, you lose your focus. But you know, what examples do they have? Dennis Rodman, Karl Malone, Charles Barkley, pitching fits, whining, arguing with the refs.

For my guys, the referees are the only explanation. They don't look at themselves. And so this becomes part of what I'm trying to teach them. And maybe it's part of what they're trying to teach me, that things are not always fair.

[playground sounds]

In our neighborhood, more than a quarter of the children live in poverty. Just look at our playground, the swings are broken, there's exposed electrical wiring in the sandbox, the basketball court is cracked, and the field is so dusty and grooved it looks like Mars. Go up to a wealthier, whiter part of the city, and the courts are smooth, the backboards new, and the fields green. So, you know, who am I to tell these kids it's a totally even playing field?

What I do keep saying is this. Look, this is the game you're in, and you have to figure out how to play it as best you can. You have to be so good that no one can call anything on you. Outplay, out-think them all, including the refs. Maybe the game is stacked against you . . . but you can still win.

Sound to Black

After the first season ends, I stop by the playground basketball court to say hello to the guys, and I begin to see that the court is one of the few safe arenas where a young man can try on his manhood. The ritual is in the challenging, the boasting, muscling, and dominating. Author John Edgar Wideman captured it in *Hoop Dreams*: "Playing the game of basketball is our way of telling stories, listening to stories, piecing a father together from them. Practicing bittersweet survival from them, whether we find them or not." I raise money for new rims, backboards, and then hire the contractors to install them. I am no longer satisfied to describe problems. I put just as much effort into solving them.

May 2001. I am on my way to the basketball court and have to sidestep six television cameramen and their portable chairs. This is how I learn that Congressman Gary Condit owns an apartment around the corner from my house. This is the same congressman who is being questioned about a missing Capitol Hill intern named Chandra Levy. Her disappearance is a big national news story for weeks, and reporters stake out the sidewalk to catch an image of the congressman. I know one of the cameramen—he grew up with me—and I stop to talk. I suggest that his crew do a story about the other children—poor African American children, who are also missing from this neighborhood. "Katie, you know what the editors will say." The next morning I write an open letter to the media asking them to cover stories of these "other missing children," and the producer of *All Things Considered* airs it.

"Wide Shot"

Turn around; focus your cameras on the basketball court, a block from the press stakeout. Ask who's missing. Few will say Chandra Levy. The kids will tell you about twenty-year-old Bai Secka, their friend, cousin. Bai died May 25th, right when the press was beginning to dig into the Chandra Levy story. His death was given one line in the *Metro* section of the *Post*—one line about a young man shot down by two bullets.

Now I can hear the press saying, "That's not a story. That happens all the time." But why? Why isn't it a story? If the press covered the murder of Bai Secka every day for ten weeks and saturated the news shows with the details—a young man with promise, who dipped into trouble and was a trying to climb out—if we covered that story every day . . . don't you think that we might come up with some new understanding of the problem?

A week ago, we dedicated our annual basketball tournament to Bai, and that morning I invited the cameramen and producers to walk the half block and take note of another person who is missing from our community. No one moved. I'm not suggesting that Chandra Levy's disappearance should not be covered. I'm just saying that out of the six camera crews down my street and their attending throngs, one or two could pan a bit wider—and take in some of the other people who are also being disappeared.

"Write more essays like that," the show producer calls to say. I try, but it turns out that I cannot plan to write an essay about an issue or news story. My work only emerges out of what is going on in my neighborhood. Months can go by with all sorts of minor events percolating on the street, but the stories must unfold enough for me to make sense of them and I can almost never peg them to national news. Other times, something dramatic happens, and I need time for the event to settle before I write about it. In 1999 two teenagers from my bike group were accused of stealing from the bike shop on Columbia Road, and I did not write the story for more than two years.

"Steal This Bike"

"Katie, we've got a problem." A neighborhood store manager was on the phone. "Your kids just stole something from us." I had sent two members of my bicycling group to buy a new wheel so they could go riding.

VOICES OF LEANDREW AND IBY: Every time I ride my bike, it's to get away from the city. I ride as far as I can. It feels good, it makes you think, and you just be riding and riding.

Iby and LeAndrew carry themselves upright in our neighborhood, so when the manager called to say they'd stolen something, I thought, Other kids, yes, not these two. "Did you see them steal it?" I asked. "No," the manager shot back, "but I have it on the security video."

A heaviness settled through me. "I'll go find them. Can you please double check the tape?" I went to the park and spread the word that I was looking for Iby and LeAndrew. I reminded myself that anything is possible. And what if they did steal the handlebar grips? Should I take away their new bikes? Ban them from our group? I decided that they would have to return what they stole and apologize. A totally humiliating experience that I went through as a kid when I got caught stealing some Brach's pink and white candies.

Back home, waiting for the boys to appear, I called the store manager again. "I checked the tape," he blustered. "It is them. . . . I'm calling the police. . . . I'm gonna prosecute." I begged the manager not to call the police. I did not want them to have any record of even being detained. "Let me handle it, please."

The boys showed up, and I gave them a prepared lecture advising them to confess. They looked at me evenly and said, "We want to see the tape." And so we went to the store and huddled around the monitor. We watched as a lone figure came up the aisle and stuffed something into his baggy pants. Iby pointed down to his fitted jeans, "See that's not what I got on." The video showed the thief in a gray sweatshirt. LeAndrew jumped in. "We had on our raincoats." The manager and I looked at Iby and LeAndrew . . . back at the video and began to see what they knew. The thief didn't look anything, anything like these two boys.

I keep thinking how we don't see each other. How we walk by, take a glance and assume so much. This manager somehow missed Iby, who has striking light skin, the color of latte foam, and LeAndrew, who has a mole under his nose that's impossible to miss.

Before I worked with kids, I did the same thing. Groups of boys, Latino and black, triggered my fear drill: grip the purse strap, don't meet the eye, walk by fast. Now I try to slow down and the two-hundred-pounder with the scull cap on turns out to be nicknamed Pooh Bear, and the sixth-grader throwing dice comes up breathless to tell me he got to play a pig in The Three Little Pigs. "Well, that's good, Moochie."

I've gained this intimacy from catching people's eyes and speaking. It's worth practicing, because if we don't see these kids, they'll never bother to see us. And when people can't see each other, they end up colliding.

This essay is interesting because of what I left out. The day after the boys were falsely accused, I called the storeowner. I knew him because he had donated tools and tires to my bike program. I told the owner that his staff needed sensitivity training and offered to have Iby and LeAndrew explain what it feels like to be a victim of racial profiling. There was silence, and then he said that he taught his staff to assume everyone is a thief. It did not feel fair to use this because I called the storeowner with my activist hat on. I didn't say that I might write a radio essay about it and quote him.

I also found that I had to let some of my own anger dissolve before I could write the story. If I had written it right away, it would have been more of a rant. I wanted to look at everyone, including myself. One footnote—a few years later Iby applied for a job at the bike shop, and the same manager who had accused him of stealing hired him and reported he was a great employee. I asked Iby if he assumed everyone walking into the store was a thief. "That's not how I am" was his answer.

These days, one ear listens as a radio producer, and one ear tries to hear between the lines of what the kids say to me as a counselor/mentor. This intimacy does not always mean I have increased access to record. Often I feel it is unethical. One day a mother called to say that a thirteen-year-old boy I mentored had been shot by a rival gang member. I had spent hours talking to this boy—call him W—about his reasons for joining the gang. I'd even recorded him as we debated the dangers of gang life and guns, with me warning him that guns and gangs are not a game. I grabbed my recorder, and I left for the hospital. I pushed the record button and walked into his hospital room. As I sat down next to W's bed, he turned to me and said, "You know, Katie, bullets really do work, just like you said."

I turned the machine off. He was speaking to me more openly than he ever had. It felt wrong to record him in such a vulnerable moment, to allow the tape recorder to keep that distance between us. He needed me to listen as he tried to make sense of guns and the damage they do. He needed to vent his desire for revenge, and I needed to talk him out of it. I never did write a story about W or the shooting. There are dozens of children I do not write about, but their voices make up a complex chorus in my head. They tell me the whys I wanted to know back when I did my ride-along with the gun squad—why does a kid need a weapon for protection? why does a kid join a gang? what is it like to mourn several friends before eighteen? I know many of the whys now, and I wait for the best ways to write about them—in hopes that my words might inspire others to listen in their own communities and to help.

I have started to think of myself as a witness-participant, keeping in mind what writer James Baldwin said—that a witness is at times called to testify. This happens to me now. I am asked to speak in community meetings, parent-teacher conferences, to intervene with cops and parole officers. I spend hours and hours with my neighbors, and that has taught me to listen differently. It is a deeper listening, and I do not always expect or need answers right away. I listen between the lines and allow events to unfold.

I know dozens of kids in my neighborhood. I know who is flirting with real trouble, who is ferrying cocaine, who is smoking weed. I have taken knives from boys, broken up fights, and I now have the street credibility to look them in the eye and say, "Come on now, do not deal drugs on your block, not with your baby cousins running around." It does not mean they stop, but the problem is out on the table for discussion and that has allowed a few of them to ask me for help in finding a real job or returning to get a GED.

I am beginning to find my own voice and place. It has been a slow crawl to my calling. I'm almost fifty now, and for the first time I feel my voice and work is authentic, and I suspect in ten more years I will really have a handle on it. The man who runs the local teen center heard my radio story about the false accusation at the bike shop, and he told me he's glad there's a storyteller in the community to gather up the threads of the many stories. That is how I've started to think of myself—as a storyteller. And I use "storyteller" in the traditional sense. I am a keeper of stories that guide. I capture the stories and keep them in trust for my community. And I retell them, and yes, sometimes I shape them.

What Did She Just Say?

damali ayo

THE FIRST WORK I MADE for radio began with an experiment about race at a very basic level, that of skin color. I wanted to uncover what people see when they look at my skin. Wearing a hidden recorder, I walked into the paint departments of various hardware stores to find collaborators in my experiment. I approached the paint mixer on duty and asked him (or, in one case, her) if he could create a paint to match any color that was presented to him. Paint mixers don't say no to this type of challenge; my next step was to present him with a part of my body to match. In succession I had paints made to match my left arm, right arm, back, belly, face, palm, thigh, and breast. I assumed the experience I was about to create with individual paint mixers would be unique, or at least interesting, so I packed up the pocket tape recorder and lapel microphone that I had bought for a previous incarnation as a counselor and headed to the stores. This was how I started making work for radio. Originally I asked a sound editor to mix the voices together for an audio montage that would play in a room of a gallery that I had painted to match my left arm, but this never really satisfied me. When Dmae Roberts called me to visit the Third Coast International Audio Festival, we worked together to create a work now known as "Paintmixers." Dmae was looking for someone to bring a new take to the conversation about race—giving stale but persistent issues a fresh appeal to keep people engaged—which is what I do for a living. She was moderating a panel on this, and asked me to sit on it with Ahri Golden, Sandy Tolan, and Jonathan Mitchell. I gave Dmae my cassette tapes with terrible sound, and she worked her magic. Every time I went to see a paint mixer I wrote about them in a journal, and we took samples from that journal to create the narration for the piece.

[NARRATION] James, left outer forearm, by scanning machine, July 15, 2:46 P.M., neutral base.

JAMES: How can I help you?

DAMALI: Well, sounds like you can mix any paint color, right?

JAMES: Just about anythang. You can give me somethin' and I'll do the best that I can with it.

[NARRATION] James was my first, and my favorite. I was nervous, but I had inadvertently worn a revealing shirt, and I think my nipples showing through provided a distraction. The paint mixers never suspected I was recording them. I asked James if he could match any color. He said yes, and I pointed to my arm. James stepped up to the challenge, saying the same thing over and over.

JAMES: I've never done a flesh tone [laughs].

[NARRATION] "I've never done a flesh-tone," which I liked because it was the first time I can remember my brown skin being referred to as a "flesh-tone." I felt I was bridging some important barrier— redefining flesh.

I have no qualms about creating a situation that offers people an opportunity to be themselves. As a performer who engages the audience, this is much of what I do, and audio is one of the most beautiful ways to capture it. This is different from typical forms of the audio enterprise, because I create a live and interactive (and therefore unpredictable) performance, and the audience-collaborator is an actor in that performance. I always say that art is only 60 percent the work of an artist; the rest is created by the audience.

I WAS BORN IN WASHINGTON, D.C., while Nixon was in the White House. The Watergate scandal launched our current epoch of flagrantly unethical role models, leaving those in my generation to create our own definitions of fairness, integrity, and honor. As I have since analyzed Nixon's behavior, it occurs to me that surreptitiously recording people, though it got Nixon in trouble, never quite struck me as the wrong thing to do. It is clear that one should avoid Nixon's mistakes by (1) not getting caught and (2) using recordings for better reasons than his. In the right hands, I wondered if recording someone without their permission might actually be a great tactic for uncovering the truth. As an adult, I tried out this hypothesis. I started recording my phone conversations. I headed to Radio Shack and explained that I wanted a simple device that connected my corded telephone and a small tape recorder. When asked why, I replied, "I'm an artist." This seems to excuse a great deal of suspicious activity, and even gets me a discount at a store or two.

Once hooked up, my device captured basic conversations, mundane moments, and the occasional profound exchange. The most memorable of which is the friend who confessed that the three most important things in his life were "music, women's naked bodies, and money." "What?" I asked. He simply repeated these priorities, adding "not necessarily in that order." I was glad I had this on tape. When it was time to challenge him on these less than noble goals, I played the tape back for him. He loved it. The idea that his words were important enough to immortalize on tape seemed to appeal to his sense of vanity. It took a few months for him to confess to me that hearing his voice had been a bit of a shock, and it was time for him to reconsider that path. Later, after he reformed and got married, he requested that I play the tape for his wife. The "good man" he had become wanted proof of the "bad boy" he had been.

He was the only one of my friends who found my tape recording even the slightest bit useful or amusing. Eventually other friends refused to call me. I had to take the tape recorder off the phone. Still looking for that sense of honesty in everyday moments, I resorted to recording myself. I talk to myself all of the time and thought that this might be entertaining to others. It wasn't. It was boring. My next inclination was to try to capture the random people who say bizarre things to me, which seems to happen on a regular basis. I frequently wish that I had tape running to record these moments. The people on the bus who ask me personal questions; the random strangers who ask to touch my hair, skin, or that strange backpack I had for a few months; the people who tell me their life stories simply because I make eye contact with them. People need to express themselves, and I seem to be a beacon for this kind of catharsis. However, I learned quickly that these moments were nearly impossible to predict, let alone capture. I simply didn't have enough tape to get it all down. Plus I felt awkward being on mic all the time; it changed the way I was interacting with people. I started to want to *create* these moments. There is a natural performer in me that brings out honesty in people, but I had to harness this aspect of my personality to generate situations that would lend themselves to tape. I realized that the best moments had to be either created or re-created.

One of the first audio artworks I made for public consumption was inspired by a conversation that took place between me and two white women friends at a restaurant in Portland. We were just digging into our salads when the Rolling Stones' "Brown Sugar" came on overhead. One of my companions said, "I love this song!" and I responded, "Yeah, but have you actually listened to the lyrics?" When she said she hadn't, I waited until the verse started and sang along:

> Gold Coast slave ship bound for cotton fields
> Sold at the market down in New Orleans
> Old old slaver knows he's doin' alright,
> Hear him whip the women just around midnight.

She had no idea that these were the lyrics. Most people don't. Few people really listen to what goes on around them, or even what they themselves say. I find that the world needs to hear itself played back.

I turned this story into an artwork by recording a re-creation of this experience over the Rolling Stones singing "Brown Sugar." Again, I sang along with the lyrics when the verse arrived. I offered a simple CD interactive port for people to listen to this piece in my show Shift: *we are not yet done.* I also made 187 brown sugar packets by hand on which I printed the lyrics. I fastened the packets to a three-by-six-foot white wood panel and let the audience read the words for themselves. My next gallery show took this concept even further. Titled *playback,* the show collected quotes and experiences from my life, or from people I know, and recontextualized them for the audience. I placed prejudiced quotes in Norman Rockwell paintings; I bought Golliwog dolls and placed them in contexts that mirrored my life experiences; I interpreted the phrase "the race card" in a series of greeting cards, a business card, and a playing card. A series of nigger jokes I collected off the web played in a video loop. I also made it possible for people to interact with my web-art-performance rent-a-negro .com, which uses my experiences and things people have said to me to explore the dynamic of race relations and diversity hiring trends in the

United States. I wanted to let people know that someone was listening to the culture we create.

At that point in my career I was a budding artist exploring the society around me and the white box of the gallery. Race and racism have always been central narratives of my life, and so I found ways to bring that experience into the gallery. My approach allowed viewers to see a more in-depth view of me and my experience as an African American woman in the United States, and at times allowed them a mirror in which to see themselves. As I grew and evolved as an artist, creating this mirror became more fulfilling and rich with potential for me. Eventually I left the gallery behind and began taking the work directly to people in any way I could dream up—into the street, onto the web, onto radio, into bookstores, onto stages, into classrooms, and even onto The O'Reilly Factor—as I explored the country's botched fascination with race.

My work consists of documenting reality and reporting experiences that people would rather overlook. People are quick to deny their actions and words, so recording them and then having the audio evidence on hand makes a big impact. I believe that art should hold a mirror to society. Sometimes society can be reflected back to itself in the simplest ways. My piece "Choose" was a play on the automated programs that assist people in setting up their voice mail when they take out personal ads.

TELEPHONE OPERATOR VOICE: If you are Caucasian, press 1; African American, press 2; Hispanic, press 3; Asian, press 4; Native American, press 5. If your ethnic background wasn't listed, or you prefer to skip this question, press zero. [Beep.]

There is a voyeuristic quality in listening to this audio. You don't know where it comes from, but its questions ring familiar as part of our everyday experience. I played it in a room full of mirrors as part of a gallery show in September 2001. Within eleven days of the opening reception, it was painfully obvious that "Arab American" was not an option on this list.

"WHITE NOISE" is a compilation of questions that white people frequently ask people of color. These questions were collected from my own experiences and those of other people of color. The audio is read by a white actress. When I assigned her the piece, she said, "Oh yeah, I know exactly what this sounds like, I grew up in Texas, and I heard this kind of stuff all the time." She improvised a few lines, which were perfect additions to the questions I had gathered. She recorded the whole litany (ten minutes worth) in one take.

WHITE WOMAN'S VOICE: Do black people get tan? What I mean is, does your skin get darker? And then do you call that "tan" or "darker"? You get blacker, right? Or do you get lighter? Do you get lighter in the sun? You speak English very well. You're so articulate. You can talk without even sounding black. But you could sound black if you wanted to, right? Do it now. Say something and sound really black. How come black people don't come to our group? I invite them. Why do you call yourselves black? I mean you're not really *black*, you're more of a brown color. Though I did see this man once who was so black. He was actually black, like the color, like my shoes. You have such an interesting name. Did you make it up yourself? Why are you always talking about racism? Can't you just relax? I tell people not to talk about race around black people 'cause you'll get really angry and call them racist. Last year I read this book, I don't remember the name, but a black person wrote it. Have you read it? You'd like it. All the black people I've met are so angry, it makes it hard to be friends with them. But you are easy to talk to. You don't get mad every time I say something. You come from a big family. And you grew up in the ghetto, I mean, inner city. Right? How many brothers and sisters do you have? Did you have to share a bedroom with all of them? Do you know your father? And you were really poor and on welfare. Or did you have money? Then you aren't *really* black. Like you are black but you are kind of white too. You kind of act white. I bet you can be black or white depending on whom you are talking to. Were your great-grandparents slaves? I just found out that my great-great-grandparents were slave masters. They owned slaves. Of course I don't think that's good or anything. I'm glad that it's all in the past now. I can't be held responsible for something my ancestors did hundreds of years ago. It was a really long time ago. Everything is different now. People are equal. I can't keep paying for things my ancestors did that I don't even believe in. What am I supposed to do, pay a special tax? A white tax?

People who have heard this recording have laughed and become angry, and many have cried. Conversations begin from the moment the audio is turned off.

IN "LIVING FLAG" I created this kind of "collaboration" with the audience by panhandling for reparations. I sat on street corners of various cities with a can marked "reparations" and a sign that said "reparations accepted here." As white people passed by, I offered them a chance to pay reparations into my can. I then paid those same reparations out to black people as they passed by. I wasn't aggressive. I didn't confront people. During the performance I offered a simple refrain to aid people in the interaction: "Would you like to pay some reparations today? You can pay right here." Of course, the tape was always recording.

[can jingle]
DAMALI: It's kinda a do-it-yourself approach. . . . You guys wanna pay
  some reparations today? You wanna pay some reparations?
[can jingle]
MAN: I'm assuming slavery of some sort.
SECOND MAN: Do you have anything to explain slavery?
DAMALI: I have to explain slavery?

A wide variety of people passed me by. The largest payment I received was ten dollars from a man in Portland who watched me for several minutes, gave me the money, thanked me, and declined the offer of a receipt. The smallest, twenty cents, came from the assistant to the contemporary art curator at the Whitney Museum of American Art. Many white people paid me money, usually their spare change, one or two dollars. One white man stood with me for what seemed like hours telling me how screwed up society is toward "minorities." When I stood up to give some money to a black truck driver, this same white man followed me and when he thought I wasn't looking grabbed a lock of my hair and rolled it between his fingers.

Lots of white people refused to make a payment, claiming, "I'm enslaved by the IRS."

Giving away the reparations payments was the best part of my days. People were surprised to get money from someone sitting on the street. Many black people came over to me because they were concerned about a young woman sitting on the street looking as if she were in need. When I explained my task to them, joyous laugher was often the first reaction. When I explained further that white people had made the payments that I was giving out to black people (I usually had to explain this part twice), their response was at first disbelief and then pleasant surprise. People wanted their reparations. It was thrilling.

More than any other moment, a group of adolescents created an experience I will never forget. Of all my audience-collaborators, I found these teenagers the most powerful—more than the white man who argued that I wasn't living in reality, or the white woman who screamed and yelled at me that I was uneducated. This group of kids (two white boys, two white girls, and one black boy) created such a compelling moment because their experience happened between them—not between them and me—because of the space created by my performance. It went like this:

DAMALI: I'm collecting reparations.
DAMALI TO BLACK KID: You, you don't have to pay.
BLACK KID [raising his fist]: Black power! [nods] All of our hard work.

The white kid standing next to the black kid pushes him, throwing him off balance.

WHITE KID: You're only half black.

The black kid grows angrier. Looking at the white kid, he points to his skin color on his arm. The white kid starts walking off. The three other white kids in the group stand and watch. The second white boy takes a step toward the first white boy. The two girls cover their mouths and mutter awkward laughs. The black kid tightens his face and his brow furrows. He frowns, then places his hands on his hips.

When those young people left me on the street corner and went back to their lives, did they continue to have that conversation? Were their friendships different because one had gotten angry and the other violent? Did the two girls who stood and watched the whole thing quietly have to mediate further arguments between the two young men? I will never know, but I can be sure that these and other questions are raised for the people in this scenario, as well as for those who experience it through audio. When people are allowed to interact with art in this way, without a narrator explaining, interpreting, or telling them what to think, the audience enters the work, moving beyond simply listening, observing, or being reported to. They start to experience.

Another memorable, and more hopeful, moment occurred in Harlem between a despondent black man and an in-touch white woman.

[NARRATION] People always ask me if my work has a sense of hope. I respond that I'm just engaging reality, offering real chances for dialogue. One of these moments happened in Harlem. A black man complained to me about white people and their lack of respect. Then a white woman came up and paid two dollars in reparations. He was shocked.

MAN [in conversation]: That's the first time I've actually heard somebody say that.

WOMAN: It's true though.

[NARRATION] He said he'd never heard a white person care about black people. He continued to listen, and eventually, he asked her for a hug. The two embraced as I watched from the sidewalk below.

Sometimes the scene wasn't quite as rosy. I found that white people are harboring a level of rage usually, stereotypically, assigned to black people. Here are a few more of the comments I recorded on the streets:

WHITE WOMAN #1: You want reparations or you want something to do with slavery, don't sit on the side of the street and bum money. It's just dumb.

WHITE MAN #2: She and her group should go to work to better themselves. Instead of trying to get reparations for past deeds to their people.

WHITE WOMAN #2: I know they were mistreated and maybe they deserve something, but to sit there and beg for it on the street corner . . . not too classy.

WHITE MAN #2: I don't think it's my personal responsibility to repair people for things that were inflicted on them a couple of centuries ago.

WHITE WOMAN #2: How can you fix that injustice? You can't . . . with money or anything else.

WHITE MAN #3: I think it's a completely irresponsible idea. We corrected the wrongs as we went along. It's un-American, it's unconstitutional, and it's dead wrong.

Something has to help us break through these patterns of ignorance, passivity, and denial. What better way than to listen to our own voices? By presenting these voices, I hope that reality becomes impossible to ignore. As an artist, my audio work has been crafted to give our society a mirror in which to observe its own blemishes. I hand the audience their reflection in the hope that they will discover the urgency of these issues and the opportunities to heal them.

DAMALI: I'm collecting reparations payments, and here—I'll make a payment to you.

BLACK PERSON: For what?

DAMALI: For the work of our ancestors . . . no, but that's what I'm doing. I'm collecting it from white people, and I'm giving it to black people. There you go. What do you think of that?

BLACK PERSON: [Laughs.] Is this some kind of quiet way of protesting or something?

DAMALI: I'm just getting the work done, you know what I mean? Getting the job done.

Out There

Sherre DeLys

I.

SHERRE: We've been traveling for a couple of hours through Yolngu lands, passing by the countries of about fifty different nation groups, each with their own languages and stories but bound together by kinship. On either side of the road—eucalypt trees, native grasses waist high, and cycad palms hinting at a time when dinosaurs roamed. . . . Yingiya tells me that his people used to travel here by foot, following winding ancestral tracks. And all the way elders were teaching . . . the names of plants, stories about their land. In our four-wheel drive we're ripping along this dirt road, and I wonder at what I'm missing.

Not that I'd ask.

This is transcript from a piece I made as my contribution to the Atlantic Public Media series *Stories from the Heart of the Land*. I recorded Yingiya Guyula and myself on a road trip to his ancestral home in Arnhem Land, 100,000 square kilometers of indigenous-owned wilderness in Australia's Northern Territory. Days earlier I'd flown on the red-eye from Sydney to Darwin, connected with a morning flight to the isolated mining township of Nhulunbuy, and then traveled by road to an escarpment overlooking the Gulf of Carpentaria right at the Top End of Australia. I came to meet Yingiya and to find out how this tribal Yolngu man, the first to earn his pilot's license, had managed in a white education system that must have seemed entirely foreign. For reasons I didn't understand at the time, Yingiya wouldn't discuss his struggles when we first met, and I soon found myself traveling still deeper into the bush. As we left, Yingiya asked if I would leave behind my "rude" nonindigenous habit of asking questions.

YINGIYA: We're just coming across the boundary of my homelands.

[sound of car stopping]

If you like I'll do my dance over here, while you're recording.

[sound of Yingiya singing, imitating bird calls, and dancing]

SHERRE: I'll never forget this moment. Yingiya does a rain dance as soon
as we arrive at the billabong here at Barmanwiliya. While I record the
sounds of wind through the red-flowering naamba trees, I think I'm
being given a lesson.

YINGIYA: The wind, the trees tell the story, that there is a spirit in my
country. It is not a teaching that you do in classrooms, by reading and
writing. You've got to be able to teach your children by *showing* the actual objects you're talking about. The tree bent over by wind, it makes
a whistling sound. It weeps. It sounds like a person, you can hear your
ancestors crying. It can be a weeping of welcoming, tears of joy. Or it
can be lonely and missing its people. It can be crying out "Come back
home and be with me." And when that happens you start to feel like
crying. Because you are teaching your children, and behind you is the
support of your ancestors. The birds might be singing out there, the
wind might be blowing around, they're all cries of your forefathers.

[sounds of birds]

SHERRE: Amazing—on other lands he's reticent. But here at Barmanwiliya, Yingiya's pride wells, the poetry flows. And I get it now that he
feels authority to speak . . . because his ancestors are here telling the
story with him. He said that before, but it didn't make sense. Not until
we were here.

A road trip to a remote indigenous territory provides a classic narrative arc
for going deep into the unknown, a trip into a culturally inscribed landscape as well as a physical journey. But more importantly the journey into
Arnhem Land gave me the opportunity to engage in a collaborative process in which Yingiya led while I followed. By taking me to his place
Yingiya did much more than answer my questions. He led me to experience what it is like to struggle to learn in an unfamiliar environment. And
the listener can feel that.

There's more. Distinct from my "ear witness" recordings of the birds and the moaning winds, Yingiya responded to their calls, displaying an intense regard for these representatives of spirit in the world. Here again I believe there's much to learn by following Yingiya's lead—for shouldn't we too, as documentarians, enter into a transformative call and response with the world around us?

II.

ANDREW: If I were a finch nesting in the children's hospital and I saw a cast around someone's leg, I'd think . . . is that a big . . . what do they call those things you find around in the beach, scuttlefish, is it? Yeah. I'd think it was a scuttlefish, and I'd start sharpening my beak on it.

While at the Westmead Children's Hospital in Sydney I became inspired by the institution's philosophy of total healing, of respect for the imagination of the child. Westmead is a hospital with landscaped gardens, an aviary, and an enviable collection of contemporary art. It even has its own radio station—"a station with a therapeutic state of mind," as Robert Krulwich put it when he interviewed me at the 2002 Third Coast International Audio Festival about my documentary "If."

SHERRE: I was at Westmead making a sound installation when I met this young boy, Andrew Salter. The hospital had commissioned me to make a little interactive piece using the voices of patients . . .

ROBERT: So Andrew comes clip-clopping down the hall, and you think "that's a nice kid."

SHERRE: No. I wanted to do something with a child there, but I didn't realize how hard it would be. Sound engineer John Jacobs and I went from room to room meeting children, and of course they're sick so mostly they're very quiet. I was about to give the idea away when we walked into a room and there was Andrew. He was up, so he wasn't that unwell at the time, and he was just so full of life and spark it was obvious—that's the kid.

ROBERT: And in your mind you needed a kid to do what?

SHERRE: Well, I didn't really know . . .

ROBERT: So you turned to Andrew and said, "Let's . . ."? What's the rest of that sentence? Let's . . . *what?*

SHERRE: "Let's go for a walk." I think we ended up in the aviary. I said, "Andrew, what if you were one of those birds?" and to my amazement . . .

ANDREW: If I was a bird and I saw a bandage around someone's head I'd pretend it was my nest and start laying eggs there.

SHERRE: I thought, Okay! So on it rolled. We walked past an aquarium. . . . "What if you were a fish?"

ANDREW: If I were a fish in the children's hospital, I'd say, "Who's in the cage, is it me, or is it you?" Well it's me, you fish.

As we walked around the hospital grounds we played a call-and-response game, with Andrew repeatedly asked to imagine himself as the plants and birds we came across.

ANDREW: If I were a plant at the children's hospital and I saw the kids go past, I'd think to myself, "I'm lucky to be a plant, seeing all these sick kids go by and I'm as fit as a fiddle. Or I might be turned into a fiddle, but I'll be fit *as* a fiddle."

Andrew's spirited wit was one thing, but he also had a lovely lilting speech. Later, in the studio, John Jacobs and I looped small samples of Andrew's voice and then recorded musician Ion Pearce following the vocal samples with his cello and voice. I love Ion's tentative striving to mimic Andrew, the delicate way he looks for a connection, the way he goes out beyond his range.

I suppose that, without thinking it through in this way, this piece exists in a space between documentary and music. At six minutes, "If" feels to me

like a kind of "docu-pop," and I think this is why it has proved to have a
long and varied life. Over the years it's been adapted into French, used as a
backing tape for a string quartet, and as a springboard for dance.

> If, If, If
> If I were a fish trying to help someone
> If I were a finch
> If I were a flame with the friend of a fish
> If I was a bird looking at the children that were really sick
> If

ROBERT: But when did the idea of "If" as a metric—"if if if"—occur?
  When you went back to your studio and started listening to the tape,
  or did you get if-fy in the moment?

SHERRE: Both. I loved his voice. He has that beautiful thing that children
  have, you know—he's singing. So I knew I would do something with
  that. Back in the studio we had all these different ifs, so we cut them
  up, made a rhythm out of them.

ROBERT: But who's the giggler? There's a giggler added on . . .

SHERRE: It's little Hannah Peters. [Laughter.]

ROBERT: Little Hannah Peters. Where is she? She's just in the back pocket
  somewhere? [Laughter.]

SHERRE: We had Andrew's voice on tape. We isolated little musical bits
  and put them on a loop, so that over and over Hannah can hear Andrew saying . . .

ROBERT: Wait a second. Do you always turn prose into verbal music? Or
  is this your first time?

SHERRE: That's the first time of doing it that way, and probably the last
  time.

ROBERT: So little Hannah. . . . If this were jazz, she'd just be sitting in?

SHERRE: She's in the studio. We're in the control room playing her these
  little segments over and over. She has her headphones on, and . . . she
  can make any noise she likes.

ROBERT: So you wait to hear the noises you need to hear? [Laughter.]
  Now you have this whole combination of sounds. What I'm really
  curious about is, how do you know when to stop?

SHERRE: You just know [laughs]. What did you think of the ending?

ROBERT: I don't know. I was just beginning to figure out that this was a
   little boy who was sick in a hospital and was imagining himself well,
   or getting better, or at least, thinking about healthy beings, fiddles,
   and fish. . . . I was just forming a picture, and suddenly out there on
   the limb of this little piece of music, I'm left there all by myself.
SHERRE: I like how you describe it.
ROBERT: *Endus interruptus*. Was that because you gave up? Or because you
   like being up there?
SHERRE: I like being up there. And a piece about "if," a piece about imagination, should be open with possibility.
ROBERT: So that's the image you're left with.

ANDREW: If I were a kid, sleeping on a bed . . .

"How do you know when to stop?" Robert Krulwich asks. The answer is simple,
I stop when I feel I've reached a moment of poise.

More interestingly though, I think it may be just such a moment that
Krulwich discovered "out there on a limb." I like to think of him balanced
in that moment, alert to it. Perhaps I'm engaging in my own wishful
thinking, but in any case I'm reminded that cultivating the potential for
active engagement is what all my work aspires to.

Robert Krulwich's playful interview provides a nice way to bring the
listener to the center of this discussion of how documentaries take form. It's
his generous and playful responses, his imaginative hearing of "If" that
I'm interested in. Krulwich is an attuned, collaborative communicator if
ever there was one, but in my experience most listeners are keen to enter
imaginatively into the exchange of energy and information a documentary offers. And if we conceive our work in ways that make room for them,
they will do just that.

But how does one actually go about this embrace of the listener in
shaping a work? I believe that when we enter into an improvised, open-
ended dialogue with our subject we've already done so by creating a tem-
plate for listeners to respond similarly.

III.

I like the Super 8 mm films of Derek Jarman. *The Last of England*, his rant on the corrosion of British culture by Thatcherism and greed, uses a bricolage of available materials—from nostalgic home movies shot by his father and grandfather to violent staged and "found" scenes of urbanized wastelands and poisoned countrysides. Elgar's *Pomp and Circumstance* vies for airspace with Diamanda Galás's shrieking gospels of disgust at society's response to the AIDS epidemic.

Unlike linear narrative films that seem complete, without need of a viewer's active interpretation, Jarman's more open-ended work deploys sounds and images through a process of structured improvisation. I wasn't surprised when I learned some years ago that this English filmmaker and painter was also a gardener.

Jarman, who died in 1994, made his final home and created his last garden at Dungeness, Kent, living in a fisherman's cottage on a bleak stretch of shingle beach adjacent to a nuclear power reactor. In 1986, during the filming of *The Last of England*, Jarman was diagnosed HIV positive. Soon afterward he purchased the derelict cottage and began a transformation of the landscape that would continue over the next eight years. I first saw the place in a book of photographs published after Jarman's death. The text, by Jarman, described the garden as "haunted by paradise," and indeed, in photographs this garden had an otherworldly quality. I became inspired to see if I could document Jarman's strange garden at the edge of the sea.

Gray, red, and white stones formed circles protecting delicate plants in this windswept place. Geometric forms made from flints, shells, and wind-twisted wood stood side by side circular plantings of sea kale, flowering weeds, and more traditional garden plants. A timber window box was filled with stones and a boat hook. The warm brown metal of sea-rusted anchors and old mines and shell cases provided contrast in a field of gray water-worn stones that formed the shingle beach, while the wind, to clangy effect, played upon sculptures created from old tools and chimes made from triangles of oxidized iron.

I spent the first day sitting in the garden and walking around Dungeness, with its boats and rusting metal strewn across the stony landscape. And I began to understand the language of the garden, this creation that had seemed so strange in photographs. In the garden Jarman had reinvented the environment around him. I pictured him on long walks taking cuttings from the wild flowers that grow in Dungeness and collecting iron relics from the coastline's history of defensive fortifications to serve as frames for climbing plants. I imagined him beachcombing for wood to build new sculptures and spending evenings assembling flotsam and jetsam, matching pieces and putting them at right angles until they were "just so."

As an admirer of Jarman's cinematic work I'd appreciated this dedicated experimentalist's methods, and here in the garden his improvisatory process was once again revealed. I love this—when I feel as if there's an invitation in a work to become imaginatively involved. And I decided to do just that, to respond to the garden in its own language. Following Jarman's lead, I manipulated recordings of the Dungeness environment to form patterns, aestheticizing and reordering nature. I made sounds using the stones, mechanical springs, and chains that form circles around the plants. I sampled those and put them at "right angles." With my friend composer Chris Abrahams along to help out, I found a process that was a response to Jarman's own.

> The TB unleashed floods of tears. . . . I weep for the garden so lonely in the shingle desert.—FROM JARMAN'S DIARIES, EASTER MONDAY, APRIL 1990

A diagnosis of tuberculosis explained the high temperatures, aches, and disorientation that Jarman had begun to experience, and there were more AIDS-related illnesses to follow. But Jarman spent much of his ever-diminishing energy over the next few years seeing the garden through its seasons; when he eventually died at age fifty-two, he left it to his young love, actor Keith Collins.

Keith moved away from the glamorous London world he and Jarman had shared, and six years after Jarman's death I found him still in Dungeness. He'd become a fisherman, and he daily tended the garden. Lines from John Donne's poem "The Sunne Rising" in wooden lettering faithful to Jarman's handwriting covered the cottage wall facing the garden, and Keith tarred them yearly to slow their decay from the salt spray. For how long would Keith stay, I wondered?

Keith brought us inside the cottage to hear the chime of a clock whose inner workings Jarman had tinkered with "so that it chimes when it wants to." Keith said he was held in Dungeness by the silence. "There's very little to interrupt here, just the wind, and the way it plays on the metal sculptures." He added that at times the sound reminded him of Derek's film *Edward II*, which starts with the rattle of a jailer's chain. And as I became attuned to the rhythms in this place, "Jarman's Garden" became, for me, a piece primarily about time.

> The gardener digs in another time, without past or future, beginning or end.
> —FROM JARMAN'S DIARIES, TUESDAY, MARCH 7, 1989

Back in Sydney, I worked with Chris Abrahams in the studio. We were inspired by the aesthetics of passing time, by Jarman's love of artifice, by his reordering of nature. What if Chris's piano mimicked the chime of the clock whose habitual intervals Jarman had modified? Because, Chris teased, what are the second, the minute, and the hour, but a painting of time? Chris was interested in referencing Jarman's films. Could he make a "Super 8 music" from sheet music found in an old book, *National Songs of the British Isles*, that would resonate with Jarman's notions of British history, family, and nostalgia?

Later, as I worked to bring the threads of sound, music, and ideas together, sometimes inviting Chris in to add a new part, I felt my way toward the form of the piece. In the final section, Keith talks about what he sees while he's out on the fishing boats.

> The things we see out there. . . . It's something called a common
> sunstar. It's a kind of starfish with twelve legs and I can't believe that
> someone first saw it and called it common, because it's the most
> uncommonly beautiful. . . . Its patterning is a fractal so that as you
> look into it, you fall into this tiny orange and yellow thing. . . .

Then, for the last six minutes no more words are spoken. There's the crash of waves rolling in and sucking back across the stones of the shingle beach. There are gulls' cries, and a hint of the bell Jarman wore around his neck when he lost his sight during the last stages of his illness. Over time the ocean waves shift from a naturalistic repetition to a metrical one. They're joined by an electric piano. The regular rhythm of hands at the keyboard pulls against the periodic tides. A synthesized "tugboat" arrives and departs. As the piano fades, it's as if the waves want to fall into time with it. And eventually the waves stop as well, sucking back over the stones and out to sea for the last time.

I LOVE WORKING WITH sound for its ability to invite listening as deep as the ocean. So many people have told me that in the rhythm of the waves in this last section of "Jarman's Garden" they hear the "death rattle"—the strained breathing of someone approaching death—that I *almost* begin to believe I intended it that way. But I'm more interested in the associations that seem to arise, that are possible, when we allow sound to settle us. Perhaps it's sound's ability to mesmerize us into a slower, stiller mode that promotes reflective inquiry. Opportunities for this way of being in the world are more precious than ever.

As a radio documentarian I'm looking for just such opportunities to take listeners out there where—like the wind weeping a welcoming through the naamba trees of Arnhem Land or rattling a jailer's chain in Dungeness—we move in the space between the spirit and the everyday, where the common becomes uncommonly beautiful.

Cigarettes and Dance Steps

Alan Hall

WALKING ALONG A LEVEE in New Orleans late one afternoon in the summer of 2006, it struck me—just as a match was struck by my companion to light his cigarette—that the smallest details in a radio feature can be the most telling. They can also be the most elusive in a form that is itself somewhat elliptical in nature. Within British radio, the feature—or documentary feature—is a subgenre of "built speech" programming, usually long form and tending to apply the techniques of fiction to factual stories. Its intention—or *destiny*, to use the words of Laurence Gilliam, director of the BBC Radio Features Department in the 1960s—is to "mirror the true inwardness of its subject."

Radio, of course, is transmitted through the air as sound waves. It affects us physically, touching our ears and penetrating our bodies, leaving auditory images that resonate in our hearts and minds. As a medium, it's both cerebral and emotional. Radio's perceived limitations—the absence of the visual dimension, its restriction to the relentless progression of linear time—disguise the genuinely uninhibited world of possibilities it offers.

A year after Hurricane Katrina reduced New Orleans to chaos, I visited the city in the company of a former soldier, William Thompson. He had been studying music at the University of New Orleans when his decision to fund college by joining the National Guard caught up with him. He was deployed to Iraq, serving in a combat unit in Baghdad. Will reconciled himself to active service by taking the opportunity to make a musical response to the sounds he encountered there. Packed away with his company's military hardware was Will's electronic keyboard. Nearly two years later, he returned to New Orleans, just two weeks after Katrina had hit, and found he'd exchanged a war zone for a disaster zone. Having come across Will's *Baghdad Music Journal*, the CD of musical sound collages in which he documented his war experiences, I was commissioned to produce a BBC feature telling Will's story. As well as Will's music and the long interviews I recorded with him, I was keen to access his raw recordings of gunfire and Humvees, calls to prayer and the soundscape of a Baghdad night—powerful audio characters in Will's story.

But it was a far more ordinary sound that became the key to the feature. In the three days I spent with him, only rarely did Will not have a cigarette alight. The sound of matches being struck and the unmistakable grating of a Zippo lighter punctuated my recordings. Driving through New Orleans, we would be held momentarily at a red light and he would light up. Peering into the wrecked interior of a jazz club where he used to play, he lit up. Faced with a question about his role in Iraq and the political forces that took him there, he lit up. After talking in his FEMA trailer for half an hour, he would step outside for some "air" and a cigarette. It was a slow burn, but eventually, on that levee, I suddenly realized the importance of this mundane action. It was both nothing and everything. In the compilation of the feature, the sound of a struck match or a lighter came to convey much more than the information that Will was lighting another cigarette. It became a key indicator of character—not just of Will himself, the soldier-musician, but of any weary soldier pictured with a cigarette hanging from his lips. And also of any musician in a smoky jazz club performing with a cigarette between his fingers or poked between the strings of a guitar's machine head or rested on the upper keys of the piano. Beyond that, this banal sound came to represent something else: the action of smoking, inhaling and exhaling, came to signal that Will was present, he was breathing, he was alive—amid the devastation of Baghdad and New Orleans—and he was taking time out to reflect upon where he had been, what he had seen, and what now lay before him. The radio feature is inherently untranscribable, but "William Thompson IV's War" ends this way:

[music, "Dim Blue Voices," solo piano crossfades with jazz trio version]
WILL [voice-over]: When I came back, one of the first things I wanted to
   do obviously was to play some piano. . . . Yeah, I'm gonna turn the air
   back on—it's a bit hot. . . . Alright, let's go outside. I wanna smoke a
   cigarette.
[sound of lighter]

WILL: It was rough. It was rough, definitely, but I kinda liked the things I
   learned about myself . . .

COMRADES ON A BAGHDAD ROOFTOP: What do you want me to say?
   What would you like me to say? What do I always say to you?

WILL: . . . having been there. Priorities—that's the main thing. Living
   your life, knowing that it could stop at any moment is a pretty beautiful thing. It was kind of liberating.

[sound of a train]

[jazz trio crossfades with solo piano]

WILL: Everything in life, the volume got turned down a little bit, you
   know. Those things that used to bother you don't bother you quite as
   much as they used to. And I think that's good. . . . I don't know.

[piano cadences, train passes]

WILL [draws on cigarette and exhales]: You've listened to the sounds,
   and you can come up with your own conclusions.

[passing train fades to black—the end]

This metaphoric elevation of the sound effect of a match might not be
consciously acknowledged by the listener. But it is heard. The ever-open ear
takes in everything and, miraculously, seems to catalogue the continuous
unconscious absorption of everyday—and everynight—sound in such a
way that each association and resonance can be released, like Proust's mad-
eleine moment, by the right trigger, the right key.

   For the feature maker, sound—pure sound—is as potent a substance as
any carefully weighed word or well-chosen musical figuration. Possibly
even more potent. It should be used with care: *no sound is innocent*.

IN A RADIO NEWS REPORT, sound is included to convey information about
the location or the occupation of the speaker or to indicate how we should
interpret the unfolding story. It's essentially illustrative and the extent of its
use tends to suggest the tone of the piece. Gunfire, like that in Will's recordings, immediately lends a report weight and urgency, though soon the
words of the reporter are likely to assume center stage. Further sound
effects, if they do appear again, will function either as punctuation, divid-
ing scenes and thoughts, or they will directly illustrate the story. The beep
of a heart monitor takes us onto the hospital ward. Crowd noises place us

on the street—perhaps in a demonstration or at a sports event—clinking glasses set us in a bar, a bell in church or school, grinding machinery on a factory production line, grinding cicadas in a southern night. The intention in news pieces is that these sounds are stripped bare of ambiguity. They are literal, informative, and unmistakable. They are reduced to their essential everyday significance. And, therefore, there's a danger they can become almost cartoonlike, not too far removed from the caricatured sound effects of comedy routines. As such, they might undermine, dilute, or distract from the real story—the information—which is being carried in the words of the reporter. There's a clear hierarchy here. The word is supreme. Sound is tolerated under controlled conditions. Music comes with a hazard warning. (Music cannot be relied upon to advance the informational narrative—it brings too much feeling, too many associations, too much bias, too great a risk of trivializing or sentimentalizing or subverting a news story.)

In the world of the everyday, sound's potency occupies the shadows between music and speech. This is why sound is so important to the feature maker. In crafting radio features, the producer is using sound not only for its everyday, informational qualities—we do not hear a match being struck only to inform us that a cigarette is being lit—but for its metaphoric qualities. These are musical, poetic, or even balletic. Sound has the capacity to take the listener out of the everyday by making images dance across the imagination. Sound offers a kind of portal through which a deeper, often inarticulate, consciousness can be glimpsed. It is with incidental and ambiguous sound that we can drill bore holes into the deeper recesses of consciousness.

IN THE MID-1990S, just a few years into my job as a music producer at the BBC, I had the chance to discover sound's potency in a feature that was at one and the same time a musical performance, a documentary, and a soundscape. "Knoxville: Summer of 1995" was inspired by the sound-rich language of James Agee's prose-poem that served as a preface to his Pulitzer Prize–winning novel, A Death in the Family. The program operated on a number of levels: it was a soundscape portrait of the Tennessee city, with a simultaneous evocation of James Agee's hometown almost a century earlier, drenched in memories of family life in the months before Agee's father died; it had documentary layers about both Agee and the composer Samuel

Barber; and it was a musical performance with the feature material con-
structed around Barber's famous setting of Agee's prose-poem. (The key
sound metaphor that unlocked the emotional narrative was a rocking chair
on a porch, on a summer's evening, "among the sounds of the night.") As
well as interviews with the city's movers and shakers, artists and residents, I
recorded the sounds I encountered on the streets of Knoxville.

RADIO: East Tennessee will be sunny and bright today; we look for tem-
    perature highs near 97 degrees. . . . It's going to be sunny for a few
    days and, I'm afraid, dry. Get those lawn sprinklers out . . .
RESIDENTS: It does get really hot here. It gets not only hot but humid . . .
[sound of sprinkler]
The kids around here are outside all the time, in this sweltering, bug-
    infested heat, they're outside . . .
It's nice.
Yeah, it's pretty . . .
Go swimming, play basketball and stuff. Hang out with my friends.
You don't have to go to school no more . . .
[sound of a sprinkler and a piano]
Because there's no rain, the temperature's in the mid-nineties to the high
    nineties, I'm gonna have to be out there every evening, watering that
    sod down.
HISTORIAN: I was thinking about the part of "Summer of 1915" that
    sticks in my mind, where they're lying on blankets in the backyard,
    and the men are watering the lawns with hoses.
[sprinkler fades to piano]
ARTIST: Well, at the heart of the language, at the heart of his theme there,
    he was trying to deal with memory. He's inspecting that area of his
    imagination, of his past, his creative search inside of A Death in the
    Family.
SOPRANO: Mainly in the middle section, when it's getting so excited, all
    of a sudden everything drops out and you're supposed to just sing all
    these high notes . . .
[sound of cicadas and piano]
. . . and if you over-sing it and put too much "blue" into it, then it be-

comes extremely shrill, and at that moment it's supposed to shimmer, it's supposed to hang there like blue dew on the grass.

[sound of cicadas; singing begins, from Barber's *Knoxville*]

BARBER/AGEE: Now is the night one blue dew, my father has drained, he has coiled the hose. Low on the length of lawns, a frailing of fire who breathes. . . . Parents on porches: rock and rock. From damp strings morning glories hang their ancient faces. The dry and exalted noise of the locusts from all the air at once enchants my eardrums.

The relationship of radio to the image is a complex and splintered one. I cannot think of any instances, in my own productions—not even in the location-specific "Knoxville"—where I have consciously tried to evoke specific images to accompany certain words or sounds. Listeners tap their own vast individual libraries of visual imagery. Each listener experiences the production uniquely.

On its own terms *no sound is innocent* because each comes loaded with associations, resonances, meanings, and metaphorical potential. But, beyond that, each sound is also capable of a creative combustion with other elements. The real excitement in making radio lies in the compiling of sound with the human voice and music—the possibility of transcending the everyday, of turning a routine walk into a sequence of dance steps.

For much of its history, radio has been a literal medium, an outlet for information and the discussion of events and ideas—the journalistic *mission to explain*. This is necessary and inevitable, but there's a danger it can deny a tradition of radio that has also always been quietly present, a tradition of a more creatively inclined programming. Rather than being merely a platform for delivering information, radio production can be considered an "art" that exists in linear time, occupying a territory that lies somewhere between the concert hall and the cinema.

When I consider my own route into radio and the ideas that inform my approach to feature making, music and film turn out to have provided more inspiration than the wireless past. Having grown up in the south of England, the heartland of the British Broadcasting Corporation, I suppose there may be something shameful in this confession. In any case, I had a fascination with documentary film, particularly the kind of shorts which were shown before the main feature in the cinemas of my childhood. It was in these factual but poetic films of the "Twenty-Four Hours in the Life of a City" variety that I discovered my responsiveness to heightened real life, to the dance of sound and music and commentary and image. Along with film, I was engaged by music, both as a performer and a listener. Then later, studying composition led me to write weak imitations of Mauricio Kagel and György Ligeti and John Cage, the last of whom encouraged us to listen to the sounds surrounding us. (It was not until I was well established as a feature maker that someone pointed out to me the connection between composing radio and composing music!)

To this day, I believe that holding a magnifying glass—or magnifying microphone—to the most mundane aspect of the everyday will reveal some sort of poetry, some sort of music. Scratch the surface of the street and reveal art. Strike a match and illuminate the human condition.

You'll be forgiven for thinking that I'm guilty here of exaggeration. A struck match, a creaking door, a ticking clock might or might not be heard to have that potency to transcend the everyday through a *musical* or metaphoric interpretation. But with the hand of the author—or *composer* or *choreographer*—placing sounds in time and within a context, the uninhibited world of possibilities begins to open up. Sounds on their own aren't enough—however Cage-ian our appreciation of them. They need a composer, a producer, a feature maker. If these elements are well composed— or, if you prefer, choreographed—a kind of alchemy takes place, a transformation of base materials into gold. This choreography responds to the rhythms of speech and the tonal qualities and pitch frequencies of voices, just as much as it does to music and pure sound. Then, in a more abstract way, it responds to the deeper unvoiced resonances of the combined elements in order to shape an emotional—a poetic, a musical, a balletic— contour.

The most emotionally delicate production that I've been responsible for was "Kindertotenlied: Song on the Death of Children." In 2003 I "composed" a radio feature about the experience of losing a child. But rather than simply report the stories of the central contributors, two bereaved fathers, my intention was to create a "monument" using the particular qualities of the radio medium. I felt justified in this approach, because everyone I spoke to for the program wanted their loss acknowledged and their children remembered. I felt, as a father myself, an obligation to gaze into the deep pain of others. Eight-year-old Evie had written poems from the moment she was diagnosed with a brain tumor. Sixteen-year-old Adam's father, a violinist, performs a requiem for his son composed by a family friend. Resonances of their stories were picked up in poems by Friedrich Rückert and the music of Gustav Mahler, who both also lost children. The key sounds in the feature were the silences between the words of the fathers. This extract is from about two-thirds of the way through the thirty-minute feature.

["Terry Riley's Requiem for Adam" and ticking clock]
DAVID: Um . . . I know that we wanted to see Adam, again . . . and we
    did. . . . And I know that it's basically an impossible situation.
[music and sound of clock]
NIGEL: Her mother was holding her, and I was holding both, both of
    them and, um, her heart was beating so fast—I'd got my hand on it.
    And it just, over a period of about a minute and a half, it just slowly
    stopped . . .
[music, clock fades out]
And she was not, not under any stress or trauma, and, um, painful as it
    was, um, I don't think we could have wished for a, for a more peace-
    ful ending . . .
["Riley's Requiem for Adam" starts up again]

To this day, I'm not altogether comfortable about re-presenting David and Nigel's "impossible situations" in the form of a radio feature—particularly, that very deliberate decision to fade out the music and the ticking clock—but many listeners tell me they found some solace in it. So I like to think Kindertotenlied has served an appropriate purpose, bringing together personal testimonies and commentary, music, poetry, and sound in a choreographed radio memorial.

I USE THE WORD choreographed optimistically. Increasingly, I'm inclined to believe that dance—that easy, fluid, confident, expressive heightening of familiar actions—is the state that all human endeavor, not just art, aspires to. We all yearn to perform in the zone, for relationships to click, for that effortless taking off from the banalities of the day-to-day. In radio features, this fluency and immediacy can best be achieved through allowing the elements—voices, music, sounds—to speak directly to the listener. A more intimate relationship with the subject is possible when there are no barriers, no intermediaries, between the story and the listener's ear. Within Britain, the form of montage in radio is still generally considered to be, in the words of a BBC briefing document, "notoriously difficult to follow." A host, presenter, or reporter "in the frame" is usually required, interceding on behalf of the subject, explaining what we've just heard and anticipating what we're about to hear. This is the pervasive manner of telling rather than showing, though I suspect stories are often better served by not placing a reporter between the subject and the listener.

Writing about music in relation to fiction in *Aspects of the Novel*, E. M. Forster identified a defining capacity that I believe can be found also in the radio feature: "Music, though it does not employ human beings, though it is governed by intricate laws, nevertheless does offer in its final expression a type of beauty which fiction might achieve in its own way. Expansion. That is the idea the novelist must cling to. Not completion. Not rounding off but opening out. When the symphony is over we feel that the notes and tunes composing it have been liberated, they have found in the rhythm of the whole their individual freedom." Similarly in radio, this "opening out" characterizes the distinction between a news documentary, in which a reporter seeks to contain and convey, and a radio feature, where the intention is to find deeper and wider resonances within—and without —the listener and to "mirror the true inwardness of its subject."

Some years ago, I was presenting a supposedly inspirational session about the potential of feature-making techniques to a group of hard-bitten news and sports producers. I had already talked about the *musical* and the *everyday* and about narrative contours and emotional choreography in terms that I hoped weren't too precious, too abstract, too distant from the experiences of these no-nonsense delegates. To finish, I played them an extract from my favorite feature, which happens also to be one of my most accomplished, "Knoxville: Summer of 1995." As I believed it was a profound piece—engaging and moving—and that my faith in it had been endorsed by a Prix Italia jury, I felt fairly robust about playing it to a group of news jockeys and sports hounds. I wanted to demonstrate my proposition that radio could sink bore holes deeply, as deeply as art even, into the human heart and mind. When the clip finished I saw one of the sports producers shrug. "SFW!" she said. I asked what she meant, "SFW?" Her reply opened up for me a chasm between, on the one hand, the world of the imagination —an understanding of the deeper resonances of things—and on the other, the everyday demands and expectations of an information-driven medium: "So Fucking What!"

The potential for such a casual dismissal is always there to greet anything and everything that appears to get above itself. I struggled to decide whether it should be dignified with a response. Perhaps, all these years later, this essay is my reply.

WHILE WORKING ON A documentary portrait of the Japanese composer Toru Takemitsu in the spring of 2007, I came upon a poem that quietly answered the sports producer and also encapsulated everything I, as a feature maker, instinctively feel about sound and its significance, not just in conveying a story but in stimulating the imagination, tapping deep into the unconscious and the conscious mind, the subjective and the objective, the everyday and the musical.

The program is called "Enter the Garden," because gardens, particularly the formal Japanese gardens of the Zen tradition, were an important source of inspiration for Takemitsu, and, beyond that literal association, the garden provided a metaphor for what he was trying to accomplish musically. Takemitsu talked about "composing gardens," about translating the spatial aspects of garden design into the temporal dimension of music, and also about achieving a musical correspondence between the fixed elements of the rocks and stones, the fleeting movements of water and falling rain, and the mutable character of plants and grasses.

Within the program, sounds recorded at the Tenryū-ji temple garden in Kyoto provide a spatial backcloth to the various voices one hears talking about Takemitsu's music (his daughter, Maki, the conductor Oliver Knussen, the pop musician David Sylvian, the film director Masahiro Shinoda, and others). This is the opening of "Enter the Garden":

[sound of photo album pages turning]
VOICE-OVER: The composer's daughter, Maki Takemitsu.
[music, a Takemitsu waltz]

MAKI [laughing]: Isn't this funny? Near our house in the mountains there is a small festival once a year. There are many stupid things like dancing and games and that year he kept dancing for, like, five hours, or something. . . . My mother and I were so embarrassed, we couldn't even watch him . . .

[music crossfades with sound of rain on leaves]

[gong]

VOICE-OVER: "Enter the Garden" . . .

[guitar music]

VOICE-OVER: "A Portrait of Toru Takemitsu"

MAKI: The composer Toru Takemitsu and my father Toru Takemitsu are such different persons.

[guitar music crossfades with sound of birds in a garden]

[Toru Takemitsu speaking in Japanese]

ENGLISH VOICE-OVER: Gardens give me energy. They provide a kind of self-affirmation. And what I like about gardens is that they don't exclude people, just as music must not exclude people.

[sound of footsteps in garden]

The garden at Tenryū-ji was designed in the Zen manner by Musō Soseki, a Zen monk born in 1275. Specifically, it's laid out to enhance the poet's ability to think, feel, articulate, and create. Each element of the garden—the paths leading through trees, water features and ponds, gravel paths and carefully arranged rocks—is experienced with the purpose of ceremonially preparing the visitor for a moment of reverie and creativity. And the sounds of the garden play the least conscious but most telling part in changing the state of the visitor from that of inhabitant of the everyday world to that of thinker, creator, artist. These sounds—birds, gong, rain on leaves, footsteps—also offer the key to an understanding of the program's central metaphor.

The monk and gardener Musō was also a poet and encapsulated in four lines what I have exhausted over three thousand words trying to express here. As I walked through the garden at Tenryū-ji, I felt the resonance of these words, and I felt Musō's experience "opening out" and offering a challenge to the sports producer. Further, I could almost visualize Takemitsu strolling in the garden, the graceful pattern of his footsteps shaping a quiet, contained dance.

> Stream sounds drown out the Buddhist sermon
> Don't say the mouth alone conveys the deepest sense
> Day and night 80,000 poems succeed one another
> And yet not a word has been spoken.

Unreality Radio

Natalie Kestecher

How I Got Started and Why in This Way

I'll be honest with you. When I started making my first radio feature I didn't really know what I was doing. I was in my early thirties, was totally sick and tired of teaching English, and was getting a graduate diploma in communication. My radio production class had been given an assignment —to make a full-length radio documentary.

Ever since hearing some obscure statistical fact that the men and women who collect coins from motorists as they (the motorists) go through tolls had the most boring job in the world, I'd been fascinated. I was curious to know what sort of person became a toll collector— whether there were any who loved their work (and why), whether there were stresses in the job, whether some lanes of traffic had particular idio-syncrasies, etc. Fortunately, I managed to interest a classmate in the proj-ect, so the two of us set off to do what we hoped would be some gripping interviews with toll collectors.

When it turned out that the majority of our interviews weren't par-ticularly gripping at all, I started to work on the story of a fictitious toll collector who had become (metaphorically) trapped by his tollbooth. The inspiration for this character came from a short Spanish horror movie made in 1972 called *La Cabina*. It was about a man who gets locked inside a public telephone booth; eventually the phone booth is removed by a truck and taken to a kind of wasteland that is full of dumped booths with skel-etons inside. So, yes, I sort of pinched this idea, but my main character is a toll collector who is psychologically trapped in and tormented by his toll-booth. Interview material was incorporated into the piece, but the main thread was the fictitious story, narrated by an imaginary toll collector and performed by yours truly.

This became the first of a number of programs I made that blurred fact with fiction. I wasn't aware that I was creating some unorthodox form or style; I just often found that it was easier for me to create characters than to find them. They told listeners things that I was sure the real interviewees believed or felt but wouldn't talk about.

Lighten Up, Carlos

Another program made around this time, for the same class but with a different classmate, was inspired by a guy who I'd taken some private Spanish lessons with. His name was Carlos. He was tidy and conservative in appearance, always serious, and I knew two things about him, that he was teaching logic at a university in Sydney and that he'd only recently come from Argentina. I was fascinated by this. I mean, why would an Argentinean come to Australia to teach logic?

Obviously there had to be a back-story . . . a troubled past. I stopped taking Spanish lessons but continued to think about Carlos. Not that Carlos, but a new Carlos who was being formed in the imagination and in discussions with my classmate Dennis Archer. Our Carlos came from Ottawa, Canada. Why? Well, it seemed only logical. He'd left Canada after being dumped by a girl named Naomi. He'd only dated her twice but imagined her to be his girlfriend. Upon hearing this, Naomi told Carlos to "lighten up." Carlos took this suggestion to heart and started to research places that might enable him to do this very thing, concluding that Sydney was the "lightening up" center of the world. So he packed his bags to start a new life at Bondi Beach, Sydney, Australia.

Having decided on Carlos's back-story, we wanted to find out what happened to him. We approached a lot of people and asked them, "What do you remember about Carlos?" Of course nobody knew Carlos (he didn't exist, remember?), so our interviewees were free to create any story they wanted. Most turned out to be projections of their own lives, desires, or failures. A surfer friend of mine recounted Carlos's failures, particularly when his lightening-up attempts included learning to surf; a single woman described meeting him at one of those blind-date dinners and thinking he was really "creepy." My father, who spent time in Siberia during the war, "remembered" Carlos as an ex-KGB agent who'd become lost and dispirited after the collapse of the USSR; my mother, a new divorcee at the time of the production, thought he was the guy she had met at a party who played "Hava Nagilah" on the comb.

It was interesting to see what people came up with when given almost no facts about Carlos. Most of them were playful and imaginative in their descriptions, and because there was no script or prompting, performances felt natural—*so* natural that they were like actual interviews. And this made Carlos real.

In recent years I've attempted to move away from a style that has sometimes been described as "mockumentary." With the exception of a fake history I wrote about making garments out of dog hair ("Knitting with Dog Hair"), I can't say that I've ever set out to "fake it." On the contrary, I try to make stories that are about very real characters and concerns. But I think there's a difference between what's *real* and what's *true*. As a young student (many years ago) I was completely fascinated by Absurdist writers such as Beckett, Albee, and Ionesco, who often placed their characters in surreal situations in order to examine universal questions and struggles.

Tailor Made

Many years ago I had a relationship with a quiet man who would create the most beautiful little pieces of furniture from the wire on champagne corks. His sofas and coffee tables were particularly sublime though they were in no way a reflection of the home that I fantasized he might want to create with me. Being allowed to watch him create his exquisite pieces of household furniture was as close to domestic bliss as we ever got, and it wasn't long before we parted ways. Some years later I visited a miniatures museum in a village in Spain where some of the work of microminiaturist Nikolai Syadristy was displayed. His miniatures, which included the smallest book in the world (.6 square millimeters) and shoes for a flea, could be viewed only through microscopes. There was a bird's nest in a poppy seed, a chess set on the head of a pin, but nearly as wonderful as the obsessively diminutive and wonderful worlds Syadristy had created, were the stories that I was told when I made inquiries about his whereabouts. I was told that he'd become fed up with small things and was now only working on enormous things somewhere in Andorra. I was told he spent most of his time these days as an underwater athlete. Whether these stories were true or not, I couldn't be sure, but as you've probably gathered by now, this wasn't a huge concern of mine. I mean, even if he wasn't off somewhere creating huge objects, wouldn't it make perfect sense if he was? Years later, remembering both of these artists, I decided to make a feature about miniatures and the people who make them.

I spoke to a man who made miniature carousels, a man who made tiny soldiers, a woman who made tiny faceless dolls and used them to perform the story of her family's extermination in the concentration camps, a woman who was breeding tiny horses. There was a recurring theme in all of their stories . . . an attempt to contain and control a sometimes overwhelming world.

Meanwhile, I was also trying to make sense of my own overwhelming and changing world. As I moved out of a marriage and a large old house, it struck me how a lack of space is often blamed for problems in relationships and how we attempt to address these problems by changing, extending, or renovating our homes. Perhaps an extra room or an added view will improve our lives. . . . If only we had more space we'd be happier. Or so the real estate agents will tell you.

Having lived in a house with no shortage of space I knew that this was a myth. A very expensive one. I started to wonder if perhaps the very opposite was true. While speaking to the miniaturists, who were gaining satisfaction and control through creating tiny worlds, I went on a search for an architect who might be interested in "subtractions" rather than "additions."

Remarkably, I found such an architect, a wonderful man by the name of Paul Pholeros who believes that the less concrete poured in an architect's lifetime the greater his contribution. He is one of the few architects that I've ever come across who seeks unbuilt solutions; he often reduces the size of homes by demolishing ugly additions and has been known to submit proposals for developments that have been knocked back by town councils on the grounds that they were too small.

While Paul's work provided me with a lot of inspiration, I decided that I wanted the story of an over-sized house to be more written piece than interview. By making the story slightly surreal as well as absurd, I hoped to create the sense of a dream world. The factuality of "Tailor Made" is irrelevant, because its messages are, I hope, very real. I am the narrator, my voice so earnest that I often wondered if listeners thought they were listening to a comedy or a melodrama. At the time, my life felt like a combination of both, and perhaps "Tailor Made" was my outlet. So much for objectivity.

> Our house was too big—its ceilings too high, its rooms too spacious, its baths too deep, its corridors endless.
>
> We lived in that house, just us two, and imagined how much richer our lives would be if only we lived in a smaller house.
>
> Despite its enormous dimensions our house was unable to accommodate any furniture. Nothing looked right, nothing felt right. Everything was dwarfed, and therefore nothing was better than anything else so it remained unfurnished. . . .

Obviously, the house was a metaphor for a relationship—a relationship that couldn't be helped by more space. In the story, the couple sell their gargantuan house in a desperate bid to improve their lifestyles. A family that aspires to change the house's

> . . . sagging yet voluptuous curves into IKEA oblongs . . .

buys it, and the narrator and her mate go off in search of a tiny house:

> We simply wanted a small house where we could contain our dreams—a small house that people would want to visit, a house that we could furnish, a house that didn't have its very own weather patterns. A house with no potential to be anything other than what it already was.
>
> We sought advice on how we might find this house with no potential, that was perfectly happy in its own skin, and that would help us to feel happier in our own skin as well as in each other's. It seemed that no such place existed. The only thing for sale was the potential to expand.

The search for the small house becomes as obsessive and futile as the search for "space." After a long and fruitless hunt, a real estate agent shows the protagonist the big old house where the story began. The house is on the market at a very low price because, like the original owners, the family who bought it became overwhelmed by its space. They are isolated and alienated, and—like the protagonist—lack the awareness that would force them to look within. The fault, of course, is always that of the house. The external.

This time, however, the narrator looks at the house through different eyes. She sees its potential to be small, and she buys her old house back and gets renovators to demolish everything but the smallest room.

The listener might hope for a happy ending, but in fact our protagonist has learned nothing despite the odyssey that she has undergone. Clearly, it isn't the size of the house that is the problem. The feature ends with a nearly exact repetition of the early description of the house, "Our house was too big—its ceilings too high, its rooms too spacious, its baths too deep, its corridors endless." But this time

> our house was too small—its ceilings too low, its rooms too pokey, its corridors nonexistent. . . .
>
> We lived in that house, just us two, and imagined how much richer our lives would be if only we lived in a bigger house.
>
> Because of its tiny dimensions our house was unable to accommodate any furniture. Nothing looked right, nothing felt right. Everything was cramped, and therefore nothing was better than anything so it remained unfurnished.

Bear in mind that the original idea for this story was to produce a program about miniatures and the people who make them. Although the "house" became the central story or narration, it was only one thread of the program, and its purpose was to allow the interviews to be presented in a way that complemented them.

Despite the motivation that architect Paul Pholeros provided with his admirable ethos, I ultimately didn't include him in the program. Somehow he felt real in the wrong way. His interview gave the feature a documentary flavor that didn't work with the rest of the material. And, too, though my miniaturists were speaking truthfully about their passion for making little things, their words worked in a way that was metaphorical and dreamlike. So while the architect became the impetus for the fictional thread of the story, he wasn't present. I ended up incorporating his interview into a companion piece instead.

In the End

As you can probably glean from what you've read so far, my process is not particularly orderly or rational. I tend to start out with an idea—in this case, to make a feature about miniatures. I then embark on the collecting or research phase, usually proceeding from the literal and ending up rather too lateral. When faced with a stack of incompatible interviews or stories, I then go into what I'll call the "torturous phase." This is the part of the process where I begin to doubt my initial idea and start searching desperately for connections. I'm often tempted to give up, but if I search hard enough, the connections emerge. I find that I'm never really comfortable with a project until I've written a story for it, even if I end up throwing it out later.

Sometimes the story I write is inappropriate for the subject material, or unnecessary, even uninteresting. But for some reason this oftentimes moribund story gives me the confidence to piece my interviews and stories together. I recently produced a program on a fairly esoteric subject—the Talmudic idea that there are thirty-six hidden holy beings in the world, always present but never identified, who by living their lives the way they do keep the world going. Without whinging too much, let me say that this was a difficult project—it's a tricky thing, documenting the lives of unidentified people. But as a way of working my way into the piece, I set myself the task of pretending (to myself) that I was one of these beings. I wrote diary entries on my attempts to do my bit to sustain our world. This practice in itself had some spiritual benefits, because by pretending to be one of the *Tzadikim Nistarim* I was a little more pleasant and helpful for a while. The diary entries in themselves were boring and self-indulgent—not intended for public consumption—but the exercise helped me give shape to all my other bits of audio. It was almost as though the diary form tricked me into thinking I knew how to arrange things.

I do find it difficult to structure things without a spine to hang them from—the individual parts have a tendency to overwhelm me. Before writing the story about the house for "Tailor Made," I had a collection of interviews—with the horse breeder, the carousel maker, the doll maker, the maker of small soldiers, and an academic. The house story not only allowed me to find a frame for the piece, but it also provided the story with layers that it would have otherwise lacked. The feature now invited listeners to ask questions of both the narrator and the interviewees. And to find themselves in the program. Why this need to tame and control? How do we get so overpowered by our lives? What makes us think that "order" will help us feel less besieged and bewildered?

You may have noticed that the beginning of "Tailor Made" was pretty similar to the end of "Tailor Made," the same disgruntlement, the same issues, the protagonist still blaming the size of her house for her problems. I'm not really into happy endings, and my stories are often circular. My heroes rarely triumph. So it doesn't seem strange for me to go back to the beginning of this essay, where I said . . .

"I'll be honest with you. When I started making my first radio feature I didn't really know what I was doing."

There are days when I still don't know what I'm doing. What I mean by this is that I don't know where an idea will lead me, and I still have to go through the same phases of development I've described above—the researching and gathering of information and interviews, followed by doubt and torturous struggle. There was a time when I resolved to keep myself out of my stories and to make straight documentaries. While I enjoyed this phase, it seems that the stories I've been making recently have me creeping back in. My New Year's resolution as a radio maker? To produce at least one "Scandinavian" documentary . . . simple yet profound, with perfect recordings and no made-up characters or stories. How I will go about doing this I have no idea; the project I'm currently working on certainly isn't it. But that's another story. Stay tuned.

Finding the Poetry

Dmae Roberts

Voices have a poetry that is
Unlike
Just
Meaning.

The way people speak
With pauses,
Stutters, stumbles, abrupt—
Eruptions and

. . . pauses . . .

And Undertones that underlie the words, raised and
Low volumes
High and Bass pitch
When people are excited or tired or perhaps

. . . lying or telling the truth . . .

This all makes a difference in the context
The meaning
Old/young/rural/urban/male/female/quiet/loud

All the variances and nuance give depth and texture to the words
    they speak.
The flow. The rhythms.
The way we over—
—lap in conversation and fill in each other's sentences.
I love listening to people speak.

WHEN I STARTED PRODUCING radio in college, I had no idea I loved sound. I knew I loved writing my own words or being onstage and speaking incredible words written by classical playwrights. But sound? At the time I was a theater major and wanted to find a way to support my acting habit. So I changed my major to journalism and learned how to write for print. I volunteered at my local community radio station and learned the most important and surprising thing in my career.

I loved sound.
Recording sound.
Editing sound.

Interviewing people I'd never have the guts to talk to without a tape deck and mic. Putting together elaborate radio theater pieces by doing live mixes on turntables, cart machines, and reel-to-reels. And using the same techniques to create personal and sound-rich documentaries. At the heart of some wild productions were the sounds of words and voices structured as in a Shakespearean play, with soliloquies and a variety of scenes with characters speaking their lines, sometimes in rhyme and oft-times in improvised free verse.

For the Peabody Award—winning *Crossing East* series on Asian American history, I had an opportunity to interview people of all ages and ethnic backgrounds.

In Hawaii, I interviewed a lot of older people about the language developed by plantation workers immigrating from Asia and Europe to Hawaii. The Hawaiians call it "pidgin" and delighted in describing it for me. But nothing could describe it better than the way they converse with each other.

In "Pidgin English" from the *Crossing East* series, Domingo and Espy, a Filipino couple in their seventies discuss what they had for breakfast. There is a rhythm to the words; it's musical:

DOMINGO: This morning I had egg and bah-cone [bacon].
ESPY: Egg and bah-cone?
I had finafle [pineapple] juice.

And then I went stirring with the stirrer,
you know that look kind of like the whipping kind.

Yeah, I whip 'em.
DOMINGO: You whip 'em good.
ESPY: I whip 'em good. [They laugh.]

This poetic dialogue is priceless. I listen for gems like these when I'm interviewing and find a way to use them in my pieces—moments when a bland interview breaks out into poetry.

ESPY: *Yeah, I whip 'em.*
DOMINGO: *You whip 'em good.*

You can hear the poetry in even something as potentially dry as a museum tour. I took a tour with Carolyn Micnihimer, the curator of a tiny turn-of-the-century Chinese herbalist's shop turned museum in eastern Oregon. She was showing me a massive metal door.

Our front door, as you can see, was well locked,
as well as a wooden bolt that went across to open it from the
    inside.
And the lock . . . [she bolts the lock] . . . also was lined with
    metal. . . .
And basically they did have fears of the outside,
whether it was American or not.
We do have one bullethole in the door.
They say the Americans would shoot up Chinatown
once in a while on Saturday night
and have not a malicious time
but a scaring time
for the Chinese.

"They did have fears of the outside. . . ." Who speaks like that anymore? I knew Micnihimer, the curator, was a gold mine because (1) she was in her eighties and had the wonderful textured voice of older people, (2) the way she spoke was reminiscent of a far-off time, (3) she almost rhymed at times. While editing and mixing this cut, I always joined in with the last three lines because they were so musical and quite thematic to the story about an herbalist living on the American frontier.

> . . . not a malicious time
> but a scaring time
> for the Chinese.

Strange as it may sound, Shakespeare's iambic pentameter is the closest rhythm to everyday English speech. People *speak* in poetic rhythm. You just have to listen for it and try to keep their form when you produce a piece.

One young woman I interviewed, Miracle Draven, talked so fast it made my head swim. But as soon as I heard her I knew she was a natural for radio. It didn't hurt that she had a compelling story.

"Miracle on the Streets" is a documentary about a homeless girl who was kicked out of her family house for being gay. Miracle lived four years on the streets and became a crystal meth addict. She turned to dealing and prostitution to pay for her habit. She talked in run-on sentences, with repetitions and swift shifts of thought. To intensify the feeling I got from talking with Miracle, I overlapped some of her monologue, repeating only a few of her phrases, and underscored it with a hip-hop beat to heighten the poetry. (The asterisk indicates the phrase that overlaps here.)

> You don't eat when you're on crystal . . .*
> . . . Your appetite is suppressed.
> That's why you get so skinny . . .
> . . . Cuz you're really—you're really—you're really just not
> hungry . . .
> You don't even notice that you're not hungry—you're just not
> hungry . . .
> . . . I think my number one thing that I always ate was Pepsi,
> always Pepsi . . .
> . . . Star Crunch, which is a Little Debbie snack, costs 25
> cents . . .
> . . . Cuz I can't spend my dealer's money, so I have to spange
> my own money . . .
> That was like all I ate.
> That was like all I ate.
> That was like all I ate . . .

With the musical beat underneath, this little speech became a song. There are beats and rhythms to how people "speak the speech, I pray you . . . trippingly on the tongue . . ." (as Hamlet says). When you spend a lot of time editing recordings of people, you begin to hear the beats of their speech.

> That was like all I ate.
> That was like all I ate.
> That was like all I ate . . .

I found that if I was holding a microphone, strangers would tell me the most intimate things—the most amazing stories. The best interviews are those that could easily be turned into a play or a film. When I asked Miracle what it was like to be a prostitute selling herself so she could buy drugs, what she told me could easily be turned into a soliloquy for the stage.

> It's not like you're getting off. It's not.
> Dude, I was not even there.
> You know, I'm thinking where am I going to go to find that dope?
> Is this drug dealer home?
> Ooh, wait, do I have that one drug dealer's number?
> It's not like I was attracted to him or anything.
> He didn't have to be cute.
> He didn't have to be skinny or whatever, and be big and buff.
> I wasn't looking at that.
> I'm only looking at your wallet,
> and that's a really horrible woman to turn into.

Dialogue can further intensify a scene. When Miracle met up with her friend, Teacup, a butch teen girl, they took me into a bathroom at the public library to show me how they prepared crystal meth in the stalls. They both were fighting the urge to sell drugs again.

MIRACLE: My biggest thing right now is I keep wanting to sell it to make more money. I don't want to use it. I just want to sell it.

TEACUP: It's easy money. I know a hell of a lot of people that use.

MIRACLE: Get your hands on 120 dollars and have 500 dollars before the day is done. Boom!

TEACUP: 500, 2,000 bucks when the day is done. I've sold 600 dollars worth of dope within two hours a day.

DMAE: What does that do to the people who take it?

TEACUP: I make sure I test it before I sell it.

DMAE: That's not what I mean—

MIRACLE: I know . . . we're hurting other people the way they used to hurt us. It isn't any quicker money, it really isn't. It just gets me closer to the stuff and makes me lose my life just a little bit more, you know. I know that.

Often you can find the poetry in what people say just by editing the extraneous verbiage. In "Angels and Demons," a docu-play about domestic violence in relationships, people were often hesitant and scared to reveal themselves. Often they tried to over-explain their feelings and actions. This is an excerpt from a woman's interview describing her thought process in dealing with her boyfriend's abuse. The strike-throughs indicate edits.

WOMAN:
I felt like maybe I asked for it.
Maybe I did something ~~to him~~.
Even though I know nothing I did~~, at this point I know that~~
    ~~nothing I did~~
warranted being beaten up.
~~Nothing I did~~ Warranted being physically beaten,
~~or even~~ warranted being touched ~~in any way,~~ in that kind of way.

MAN:
When everything would get too much and I would get mad and
    let loose~~, what would end~~
~~up happening is~~ for four or five seconds I wouldn't feel
    anything.
It was just like a white out. ~~And usually during those three or~~
    ~~four seconds~~
I would be breaking something,
slamming something against the wall,
pushing somebody if it was my wife.
~~If it ended up happening like that.~~

On three of those occasions I slapped her or pushed her.
And then something broke and it was all gone.

For a year, I worked on a documentary/outreach project in which I worked
with more than thirty women to talk about their experiences with breast
cancer. We worked on outreach activities like painting, writing, and interviewing, and they told their stories. Some were recorded and some were
written pieces performed by actors. In this short clip from "The Breast
Cancer Monologues," three women are telling one story. This is a technique
I like to use to create a sense of dialogue by overlapping monologues in
which people finish each other's sentences to create a narrative.

ELAINE: You're going to what?

OLGA: They told me to crawl on the table, lay flat, and stick my breast
    through a hole.

CAREN: They had to be kidding.

OLGA: The surgeons wanted to do a biopsy to see if I had breast cancer.

ELAINE: It was cold in the hospital gown, and my body tensed at the idea
    of dropping anything as vulnerable as my breast through a hole to be
    poked, prodded, sliced by doctors below me whom I'd never met and
    couldn't see.

CAREN: They numbed my breast, and on the other side of the table I felt
    the tugging, the pressure, something like cutting.

OLGA: I wanted to cry but I pressed my cheek hard against the board.

ELAINE: I didn't dare move.

"The Breast Cancer Monologues" was performed with three actors, but it's
a production technique I like to use with interviews as well, especially if
you can get people to tell their viewpoints of the same story and then
inter-cut their comments into a montage. The following is from "Sisters,"
which traces three generations of sisters. This pair of sisters were in their
seventies and were interviewed together. They often overlapped their
speech, but I used editing to strengthen that sense of connectedness.

WOMAN 1:
From the time we knew anything about playing
we played together, built houses,
fell down steps. Everything like that.

WOMAN 2:
Our mother dressed us alike,
and they thought we were twins really . . .

WOMAN 1:
Our tastes are the same. . . .
Course I like music better than Ruthie does.
She goes to artist shows.
I don't enjoy those very much.

WOMAN 2:
We like to walk.
We like to be out.
We love nature and we love animals.

WOMAN 1:
We just respect each other's wants, and Ruthie tries to do what
    pleases me and I try to please her.

WOMAN 2:
That's all you can do.
Right now is all you have anyway . . .
particularly when you get our age.

They're telling the same story, their story, but because there are two of
them speaking, their voices interlacing, there's movement and theatricality
to the story.

DIALOGUE IS ALWAYS a fun and surprising way to begin a radio piece or to
transition to another monologue. It breaks up the pace and indicates a
refreshing movement to another section, much like a coda in a piece of
music. It's even more intriguing if the dialogue incorporates a non-main-
stream style of speaking.

Because I'm a mixed-race Asian American, I grew up with a couple of
different languages. I came to the United States when I was eight years old,
and I spoke Japanese and Taiwanese and not much English. My dad made
our household speak only English so I would forget my first two languages, and it worked. When my mother and her friends would speak in

Taiwanese, I could almost follow their conversation just by listening to the sounds and tones of what they were saying. That's probably why the way words sound is almost as important to me as the content of the words. I've never quite believed the actual meanings of words as much as their undertone and subtext.

Radio allowed me to explore the sound of words and language in a way I had never experienced before by melding poetry and sound. And I soon came to weave my experience with my documentary work. I found that I loved using actors to read historical narratives or flashbacks and to play characters that you couldn't possibly interview. Somehow that brought me closer to the truth than just relying on the memories and perspectives of interviewees. Most of the time, interviewees don't tell you all of the truth. They hold some things back. This is even more true when interviewing family members, or when doing a personal piece and pondering just how much you might tell.

Throughout my childhood, I heard bits and pieces of my mother's story, usually when she was depressed or angry. She grew up during World War II, and her parents sold her to work as a servant/adopted daughter to some abusive parents. When my mother and I took a trip to Taiwan together—during the making of "Mei Mei, A Daughter's Song"—our already tempestuous relationship got even more difficult.

For a month I recorded any sound I encountered in Taiwan. Firecrackers, Chinese opera, puppet shows, vendors shouting in a marketplace, people singing at temples, street noise, children's choirs, funerals, TV shows. I ended up with thirty or so ninety-minute cassettes rich with stereo sound. I didn't know what I would use, but I knew I would use small bits from most of the sounds because I wanted to create lots of scenes and transitions. I don't generally plot out my scenes ahead of time, but especially when I'm traveling I try to fill my time with experiences and sound possibilities as well as interviews. Then I go back and listen and dub and figure out my best bits. Then I'll write a script and start shaping it. Always it's the sound and intriguing interviews first, and then comes any written essay or narration.

The most difficult thing about recording in Taiwan was interviewing my mother, who angrily resented my questions. It was like pulling teeth to get her to say anything, and even then she cut off the interview after twenty minutes and wouldn't let me do it again.

MOM: I was thirteen and fourteen. I tried suicide three times.

DMAE: How?

MOM: Tried to hang.

DMAE: You tried to hang yourself?

MOM: Yeah.

DMAE: Three times?

MOM: Yeah. And Buddha's come and stop me. Buddha gave me power.

DMAE: How did she stop you?

MOM: I don't know how to explain it! She come down here.

DMAE: Did you actually tie a rope up?

MOM: Yeah, and Buddha come down and turned me loose.

DMAE: You were hanging?

MOM: Yeah.

DMAE: And she turned you loose?

MOM: Buddha come down and stop me.

DMAE: Did she say anything, do anything?

DMAE: Yeah.

DMAE: What did she say?

MOM: She told me that I have a long way to go.

So I took that torturous interview and wrote a monologue telling the story from the perspective of Mei Mei as a young girl. Because my mother didn't really want to tell me the story, she sounded angry throughout the interview. I felt I could get closer to the truth of her past experiences and how she survived them by having an actor portray her when she was younger. Someone who would tell her story more objectively—in the way she might tell it to a stranger, not a daughter she resented.

> MOM [as a young woman]:
> I was hanging and Buddha stopped me.
> Buddha gave me power. She said, it's not your time yet. . . .
>
> The first time I tried to kill myself, I was thirteen years old.
> I tied a sheet to the ceiling in a circle.

I put my head in the circle.
I was hanging and Buddha stopped me.
I was hanging and Buddha stopped me.
Buddha gave me power.

I chose to write my mother's narrative as a young girl as a poem. Because in real life she spoke English in phrases rather than complete sentences, using a poetic style for her narrative made sense to me. I wanted to keep the cultural character of her words and the feelings of difficulty in telling her personal story.

MOM [as a young woman]:
My real parents sold me.
They were poor.
I was two years old in Chinese age,
one year old in American time.
I was sold twice. Twice I was sold.
The first parents were not unkind.
Were not loving.
Were not unkind.
Again, I was sold.
Sim-bua—
in Taiwanese. Sim-bua—
Adopted daughter-in-law.
Sold to marry the son in the family.
I was twelve.
Sim-bua.

There were certain phrases I used as repetitions for transitions, thematic tag lines, and codas.

MOM:
We talk the Chinese, you don't understand.
We talk the Taiwanese, you don't understand. . . .

A good documentary, a good radio piece, prompts understanding on a deeper level than the written word. Because we delve into human experience—and the human voice—we convey something that's more than facts and stats. To listen to someone telling a story is to make an emotional connection. For me, radio storytelling is about sounds and words, the moments when words spoken spontaneously have a music of their own.

The rhythm and flow—
the textures and tones—
our overlapping conversations—
interruptions as we fill in each other's sentences—

and the meanings behind our words.

Good radio, like good theater, is a collection of scenes that interweave voices and sounds through monologues and dialogues and soundscapes. And beneath it all is the poetry that gets us closer to that elusive heartbeat we call truth.

Diaries and Detritus

One Perfectionist's Search for Imperfection

Joe Richman

HERE IS A STORY about a cough.

It was 1963, in a stuffy courtroom in South Africa, during the trial of Nelson Mandela and other anti-apartheid activists for treason. The prosecutor was just beginning his opening statement when somebody in the courtroom coughed. It was an ordinary cough; it lasted less than two seconds. The prosecutor's words—and the cough—were recorded onto a reel-to-reel tape. At the end of the trial, Mandela and the other defendants were sent to prison on Robben Island. The tape was sent to the basement of a government archives. It remained there, mislabeled and probably unheard, for more than four decades.

Making radio presents a simple challenge: re-creating reality with words and sound. If the story is too clean and perfect, the messiness of life gets lost. Often the most "real" moments can be found in the margins and jagged edges, in the audio detritus. An important speech, for example, may be recorded and saved, but left out of this official transcript of history is the anticipation of the crowd, the feedback of the microphone, or the clearing of the throat before the speaker begins. These are the brief backstage glimpses—unofficial, accidental, mundane bits of sound—that help a radio story come to life and pierce the armor of our memory. Sometimes these moments can be just two seconds long.

I spent the summer of 2004 rummaging through archives in South Africa looking for sound that would help tell the history of apartheid for our series *Mandela: An Audio History*. One day I pulled out a reel-to-reel tape that was in bad shape. I had to keep splicing the tape back together as it played. I soon realized I was listening to a recording from Mandela's trial in 1963. It was thrilling to hear the prosecutor's actual words. But it wasn't until the moment when somebody coughed that I could suddenly hear the echo and dimensions of the room, the stillness of the hot afternoon, and the hushed anticipation of the trial. The cough put me in that courtroom.

"Punctum" is a photographic term, but we should steal it for radio. "Punctum" is defined as a point or the precise location of something. But in photography (courtesy of Roland Barthes's *Camera Lucida*), punctum is the unintentional detail that "fills the whole picture," the lucky accident that helps us understand the true nature of a story, or a person. Recently, I saw a photo in a newspaper of a young woman visiting the grave of her husband who had been killed in Iraq. In the photo, the woman is lying barefoot on the grass, almost hugging the ground. She doesn't look especially mournful, just quiet. There is something routine and ordinary about the scene that makes it even more poignant. The photo haunted me, and I cut it out. A few weeks later I looked at the photo again, and I noticed a detail I was not conscious of before: Next to the woman, along with her shoes, a vase of flowers, and a small American flag, is a disposable bottle of water. That juxtaposition of common and cosmic, the eternal and the everyday—the water bottle got to me.

In photography, punctum is a detail. In radio, a temporal medium, punctum can be a scene or a moment, as short as a cough or as long as a conversation. You can't create or plan punctum, you just have to recognize it when it happens. That's not always easy. The moments on the edges are the easiest to miss, the hardest to work with, and the first to be edited out. But every so often you stumble on a small, odd moment that you fall in love with, that amuses you, or that haunts you. And when you find it, you have to fight with your editor, and yourself, to keep it in the story.

Audio Diaries—Looking for Lucky Accidents

At Radio Diaries, the small nonprofit production company I founded in 1999, we give tape recorders to people and work with them to document their own lives. The diarists typically record for around a year, often collecting more than forty hours of tape: sounds, scenes, conversations, and late-night thoughts. All this tape is edited and shaped into documentaries for NPR's *All Things Considered*.

Over the years I've done diaries with inmates and guards in a prison, elderly people living in a retirement home, an illegal immigrant, a judge, and teenagers of all types. One of my first—and still one of my favorite—diaries was with Josh Cutler, a sixteen-year-old with Tourette's syndrome, a neurological disorder that causes involuntary verbal and physical tics. What made Josh a great radio diarist was that I never knew what he was going to say next. Sometimes he didn't either:

> People are always taught to think before they speak. Everybody has deep dark things that they don't want people to know they're thinking about. [Scream.] The bottom line is sometimes I actually have to teach myself not to care. I can't care because most of the time I can't control what comes out of my mouth. I control what comes out of my ass better than I control what comes out of my mouth. But the last thing I want people to think is, "Oh, poor Josh." It's not like I'm in a wheelchair or I have snot dribbling down my chin. I really just don't want anyone to be feeling sorry for me. This is not a Sally Struthers commercial.
> —FROM JOSH'S DIARY, "GROWING UP WITH TOURETTE'S"

The fact that Josh could not always control what came out of his mouth is a kind of metaphor for this type of documentary journalism. The process of going through hours and hours of raw audio diary tapes is like mining for gold. Ninety percent is junk, but then every so often there are little magical moments that are completely unexpected. Details emerge about people that, in an interview, I would never have thought to ask about. Scenes happen on tape that I would never have known to even look for. Lucky, happy accidents.

In documentaries, the key to getting lucky is time; spending enough time for people to trust you with their stories, hanging out enough so that you're there when things happen. By turning the tape recorder into a constant companion, the diarists take this process a step further. It's like bringing the microphone backstage, to a place where truth and understanding are found not just in words but between words—in the pauses and accents, in the sighs and silences.

Teenagers are good diarists because they have an abundance of time. It's also an age when people are just beginning to discover themselves and their world. They are curious, and impatient for their life story to begin. And unlike many adults, teenagers have an inherent belief that whatever they say is important and people should be listening. When I ask a teenager to carry a tape recorder around for a year, they don't think I'm crazy.

Over the past decade I've lost, rather than gained, confidence in my ability to predict who will be a good diarist. I used to look for good talkers: extroverted, funny, energetic personalities. I call them talk-outers. Now I am often more drawn to talk-inners, voices that are soft and intimate, that make you lean in closer to your radio to hear what they have to say. The best diarists are a bit of both.

Radio is the perfect medium for diaries. The equipment is inexpensive and easy to use. A microphone is less intrusive than a video camera, so people can be more natural, more themselves. It takes a lot of time and practice to be natural. With all the diarists there comes a point, usually after a few weeks of recording, when they get bored. That's what I'm waiting for. They're no longer trying to sound like Tom Brokaw. They relax and become themselves.

It's like a photographer who takes beautiful portraits that are just a little bit . . . off. A photographer who doesn't snap the picture when you are expecting it. She waits a few beats until subjects begin to lose their pose, when the smile starts to slack, when they let their guard down, or get a bit uncomfortable. That moment happens in radio, too. And it's when you get the most interesting and authentic tape.

I think the real value of doing audio diaries is simply that the diarists can record things you can't. Most diarists find it easiest and safest to sit in their room and talk . . . like writing in a diary. But the real magic is when they record things happening on tape, when conversation or scene or action unfolds in a way that lets the listener experience life along with the diarist. If you manage to get just a few intimate and true moments like that into a story you're doing pretty well.

Cristel was eighteen when she began recording her diary inside a juvenile detention facility in Rhode Island. Late one night, while Cristel was recording, she heard a faint tap on the wall from the cell next door. It was a thirteen-year-old who had just recently been locked up. Neither of the girls could sleep. So they took turns knocking on either side of the cement wall, tapping out syncopated rhythms for the other girl to repeat. After about ten minutes the knocking stopped. Then Cristel picked up the tape recorder, walked over to her window, and brought the microphone close to her mouth:

> Sometimes, you know, I look out the window and I just sit here and think:
> Something I decided in ten minutes changed my entire life. Not even ten minutes.
> I mean three years have gone by, and I'm still sitting here. What would I be
> doing if I was out? What would my life be like? Would I have finished school?
> Would I have settled down? Would I have done something worse? I just look out
> the window and I think about all this stuff.—FROM CRISTEL'S DIARY FOR
> THE PRISON DIARIES SERIES

To hear Cristel speaking quietly into a tape recorder late at night, it's almost possible to enter into her world, to imagine ourselves in that cell. Moments like these can't be captured by an outside reporter. There are some stories that can only be told by those who live them.

Diarists play two roles, subject and reporter, and negotiating the two can be tricky. So the rules—my rules, anyway—are different from those of traditional journalism. I give each diarist final editorial control over their story. This allows them to record as honestly and unselfconsciously as possible; they don't need to worry about censoring themselves in the moment if they know they'll be given an opportunity to edit later. I also pay most of the diarists a small stipend for their work. These ground rules are no different from those in any newsroom when you consider that the diarist is the reporter and I am the producer. Although, usually, I feel more like a midwife.

For many people, one of the few things they have control over is their own story. Removing the professional filter of a scripted reporter or host allows the diarist to communicate directly and intimately with the audience. This is why I believe audio diaries are uniquely valuable for telling the stories of those who are marginalized, forgotten, and voiceless.

I FIRST MET Thembi Ngubane in 2004. She was nineteen and living in a shack in a township outside Cape Town, South Africa. I was interviewing a few dozen teenagers with HIV/AIDS. But, at the time, I wasn't sure I really wanted to do a diary on such an overwhelming and heartbreaking topic. Then I met Thembi. She told me how she starts every morning by looking into the mirror and talking to her HIV virus; she called it her "HIV prayer":

Hello HIV, you trespasser. You are in my body. You have to obey the rules. You have to respect me, and if you don't hurt me, I won't hurt you. You mind your business, and I'll mind mine. Then I'll give you a ticket when your time comes.
—THEMBI NGUBANE, FROM "THEMBI'S AIDS DIARY"

I realized this would not be a documentary about AIDS, it would be a story about Thembi. She was—and still is—my window into an incomprehensible epidemic. She's also my reminder about what diaries do best.

No country is more affected by AIDS than South Africa. Yet journalists there, and all over the world, have a tough time getting people to pay attention to the issue. The editor of a newspaper in Soweto told me that every time they have a story about AIDS on the front page they can expect a drop in circulation of ten to fifteen thousand papers (more than 10 percent).

People feel differently about an issue—AIDS, prison, immigration—when it affects someone they know and love. I picture a person driving home from work, listening to NPR, with Thembi or Cristel or Josh in the passenger seat. It's not me in the car telling the listener about Thembi. It's Thembi. And by the end of the story, maybe the listener feels like Thembi is somebody they have gotten to know and now care for.

How do you turn a statistic into a real person? How do you make listeners love or understand your characters the way you do? How do you bring the audience into the story and let them experience it for themselves? The key lies in the poetry of the everyday. A cough in the courtroom, a soft knock on a prison wall, a teenager's prayer as she looks in the mirror. The stuff on the edges. The irony is that often the scenes that feel the most natural, ordinary, and raw actually require the most editing and crafting. You have to be a perfectionist to capture the messiness of life.

There is one particular moment like this in Thembi's diary that taught me an important lesson, a lesson I keep having to learn over and over. In the scene, Thembi and her boyfriend, Melikhaya, are at home. He puts on some music. Thembi says, "Let's dance." She talks about how hard it was to tell him the news when she first learned she was HIV positive. And as the music fades, she asks him a question.

THEMBI: Melikhaya, do you ever wish that maybe you would have never met me?
MELIKHAYA: No [laughs], just because the only thing is that I love you. You know that?

THEMBI: Yes, but I am the one who has infected you.

MELIKHAYA: I don't want to blame you. You didn't chase after AIDS. You didn't go to the top of the mountain and say you want to have AIDS, you know? And I don't want you to blame yourself. Just be strong.

In an early draft of the documentary, the scene ends here. It felt "moving" to me at the time. But as I was listening through some old tape I discovered a part of their conversation that I had previously edited out. For some reason it had seemed too peripheral, or too frivolous, or too imperfect to make it into the story. But when I put this moment back into their conversation, it turned an overly earnest and humorless scene ending into something playful, surprising, and much more powerful. Now, these are probably my favorite thirty seconds of Thembi's diary.

THEMBI: For me, what scares me most is I think we are not going to die at the same time if we die.

MELIKHAYA: I know that you think that if you die first I'm going to have another girlfriend. [They both laugh.]

THEMBI: No! [laughing] No! Really I'm thinking if one of us dies, how would it be. At least if we were going to die [Thembi and Melikhaya speak simultaneously], die at the same time [laughs].

MELIKHAYA: Give me a kiss for that.

[kiss]

Two teenagers joking about death. It's that juxtaposition of eternal and everyday, silly and profound. It's one of those throwaway moments that, at first listen, didn't seem to say much. But in the end, it says everything. I thought it was an imperfection. I had to rediscover, once again, that there are some magical imperfections that, while hard to recognize, are worth searching for.

Living History

Stephen Smith

WHEN IT'S DONE WELL, history on the radio is like a ride in Mr. Peabody's WABAC Machine: you end up somewhere you've never been before and meet characters you never quite imagined—and it's all in color. To explain: on the 1960s television cartoon show *Rocky and Bullwinkle*, the canine genius, Mr. Peabody, would instruct his pet boy, Sherman, to set the machine for a given date. A big "danger" sign on the WABAC (pronounced "wayback") suggested time travel was no trifling matter. The pair would wander across the centuries getting in scrapes and meeting historical characters like Cleopatra, Ludwig van Beethoven, and Calamity Jane. Most episodes concluded with a dreadful pun, like "Captain Clift is from Dover. Haven't you heard of the white Clifts of Dover?"

Using cartoon as metaphor only goes so far because much of history is not very comical. But whenever possible, a vivid sense of "being there" is the objective for radio history programs. A powerfully crafted history piece transports the listener to distant, imaginative terrain the way great travel writing delivers the reader to faraway lands. The writer Bill McKibben calls radio "mental travel." Archival tape and first-person narratives are the booster rockets of radio's Wayback Machine. Tape blasts the listener into another time.

As a producer, I prefer to journey through twentieth-century American history using found audio objects and interviews with people who lived through the events. However important a theme or an idea may be, stories and characters drive the narrative, not scholarly debates. Psychologists say that the stories we tell about ourselves are a critical and ever-changing facet of self-knowledge. And, as every great history teacher knows, a good story will stick with us in a way that facts and dates do not.

Some might say we are built of stories. At the very least, we are changed by stories.

"A sense of the past is a way of being in the present," writes historian David Harlan. Harlan suggests that the power of a good narrative is its capacity to make us care about people we don't know. By projecting ourselves into their lives we may shift our own perceptions and desires. Historical characters and their stories become part of our own narrative.

IN 2003, I co-produced a documentary called "The President Calling" based on the secretly recorded phone conversations of Presidents Kennedy, Johnson, and Nixon. The tapes are stored in the National Archives and are public records. Each president had his own reasons for taping his conversations and phone calls, and none of them thought the recordings would ever be made public. The tapes offer a rare and selective view of life in the White House—a journey past the rope line of textbook history.

One story we told in the program was about Lyndon Johnson's first days as president. LBJ took office in 1963 when President John F. Kennedy was assassinated. As president, Johnson was a prolific user of both the telephone and his secret taping system. Of all the people Johnson reached out to in the first weeks of his presidency, few were more important to him than the widow of the slain president, Jacqueline Bouvier Kennedy. The two had traded letters since JFK's funeral, and on December 2, 1963, President Johnson called her from the Oval Office. Mrs. Kennedy and her children were still living in the Executive Mansion. Listeners got to eavesdrop on their conversation.

JACQUELINE BOUVIER KENNEDY: Mr. President?

LYNDON BAINES JOHNSON: I just wanted you to know you were loved, and by so many and so much—I'm one of them.

KENNEDY: Oh, Mr. President, I tried, I didn't dare bother you again. But I got Kenny O'Donnell over here to give you a message, if he ever saw you. Did he give it to you yet?

JOHNSON: No.

KENNEDY: About my letter? That was waiting for me last night?

JOHNSON: Listen, sweetie. Now the first thing you got to learn—you got some things to learn—and one of them is that you don't bother me, you give me strength.

KENNEDY: But I wasn't going to send you in one more letter. I was just scared you'd answer it.

JOHNSON: Don't send me anything, don't send me anything. You just come over and put your arm around me. That's all you do. And when you haven't got anything else to do, let's take a walk. Let's walk around the backyard. And just let me tell you how much you mean to all of us, and how we can carry on, if you give us a little strength.

KENNEDY: But you know what I wanted to say to you about that letter? I know how rare a letter is in a president's handwriting. Do you know that I've got more in your handwriting than I do in Jack's now? And for you to write it at this time and then to send me that thing today, and you know, your Cape announcement and everything.

JOHNSON: I want you to just know this—that I told my mama a long time ago, when everybody else gave up about my election in '48, my mother and my wife and my sisters, you females got a lot of courage that we men don't have. And so we have to rely on you and depend on you, and you got something to do. You got the President relying on you. And this is not the first one you had. So there are not many women, you know, running around with a good many Presidents. So you got the biggest job of your life.

KENNEDY [laughing]: She ran around with two Presidents, that's what they'll say about me. OK. Anytime.

JOHNSON: Goodbye, darling.

KENNEDY: Thank you for calling, Mr. President. Goodbye.

JOHNSON: Goodbye, Sweetie. Do come by.

KENNEDY: I will.

This conversation is both important and weird. It vividly demonstrates LBJ's intense campaign to win the approval of JFK's family, especially his widow. In his early days in office, LBJ fretted that his presidency looked illegitimate in the eyes of the world. Johnson hoped the backing of Mrs. Kennedy, and of Attorney General Robert F. Kennedy, could help change that. At the same time, the exchange reveals Johnson's sometimes peculiar style with people. His manner with the young widow is both fatherly and oddly flirtatious.

By focusing on the phone calls of the three presidents we presented a rich picture of how these powerful politicians used one-to-one persuasion to make policy and set the course of history. In LBJ's case we concentrated on the transition phase of his presidency, the war in Vietnam, and the larger-than-life nature of his character. Johnson could sound pretty dry delivering a presidential speech. On the phone he was bawdy, passionate, and often extremely pushy. This story was ideal for the radio because the tonality and pacing of human speech carry a whole subtext of meaning that can get lost on the printed page.

For our segment on Richard Nixon we interviewed historian Stanley Kutler, one of the world's foremost experts on the president and the Watergate scandal. Kutler sued the federal government for the release of Nixon's secret tapes and has written several books based on them. Among the many remarkable stories Kutler found by listening to the tapes was the way Nixon handled firing his two closest aides, Bob Haldeman and John Ehrlichman. On April 30, 1973, Nixon delivered his first nationally televised address about the Watergate break-in and the firings. As was his custom after all of Nixon's TV appearances, the just-sacked Haldeman dialed the president. What Nixon said to Haldeman stunned Stanley Kutler.

RICHARD M. NIXON: But let me say you're a strong man, goddamnit, and I love you.
BOB HALDEMAN: [nervous laugh] Well—
NIXON: And I love John and all the rest, and by God, keep the faith. Keep the faith. You're going to win this son of a bitch.
HALDEMAN: Absolutely.

Kutler says that when he first read the transcript of this conversation he could not believe that the tough, scheming Richard Nixon had professed his love for his two political aides. When Kutler then *heard* the recording, the sound of Nixon's voice explained it all. The president's speech was slurred. At points in the conversation you could even hear what sounded like the tinkling of ice in Nixon's glass. The man was tipsy. Sound told the story. We described this episode in "The President Calling." In the program, Kutler's play-by-play threaded through the archival tape.

STANLEY KUTLER: He's feeling isolated, he's feeling lonely. He starts off, complains to Haldeman, "Nobody's called me!" And Haldeman very quietly says, "But you left orders that no calls were to come through."
RICHARD M. NIXON: I don't know whether you can call and get any reactions and call me back.

KUTLER: He says to Haldeman—like nothing has happened—he says, "Can you go out and check the reaction to the speech?" And Haldeman says, "I think not."

NIXON: Well, would you mind?

HALDEMAN: I don't think I can. I don't—

NIXON: No, I agree.

HALDEMAN: I'm in kind of an odd spot to try and do that.

NIXON: Don't call a goddamn soul. The hell with it.

KUTLER: He says, "I understand," and so forth. Actually, he understands but he really wanted him to do it.

NIXON: . . . God bless you, boy. God bless you. I love you, as you know.

HALDEMAN: Okay.

NIXON: Like my brother.

HALDEMAN: Well, we'll go on and up from here.

NIXON: All right, boy. Keep the faith.

HALDEMAN: Right.

When you hear the voices of people like Lyndon Johnson and Jackie Kennedy, or Richard Nixon and H. R. Haldeman, stories unfold in Technicolor.

I'M NOT SURE HOW I first got interested in history. I don't recall any influential social studies teachers in grade school, and all I can remember about my high school history teacher is that he admired Woodrow Wilson. But my parents had a set of Time-Life books called *This Fabulous Century* that I pored over as a kid. Each volume chronicled a (mostly American) decade. I was captivated by the photographs of Dust Bowl farmers and the *Hindenburg* disaster and by the blurry snapshot of an electric chair execution captured by a camera strapped to the photographer's ankle. I also liked reading about celluloid cowboy Tom Mix and the secret decoder ring and invisible ink pens offered by his fan club (why a cowpoke needed espionage tools didn't puzzle me at the time).

I also remember reading *Huckleberry Finn* at YMCA summer camp. The story was so absorbing I skipped lanyard-making to sit under a tree and travel the Mississippi with a boy about my age (Huck was thirteen). Part of what captured me was seeing my friends and me in Twain's story. We seemed to have a lot in common with these American kids who lived a century earlier (boyish capers, clueless parents, bafflement about girls). *Huckleberry Finn* felt like time travel. The characters and stories drew me into a distant world. As an adult, what appeals to me about history—in addition to the adventuresome pleasures of the WABAC machine—is that I'm always puzzling over how we got to where we are today.

Because I like to combine first-person narratives with the primary materials of American history, I concentrate on the twentieth century. That's where the recorded sound is. There's a kind of continental divide in historical documents—it's right around 1877. Before then, events were captured in sketches, photographs, official documents, written narratives, and the like. After that date, history flows towards the modern age of sound recording.

In 1877, Thomas Edison captured sound on a cylinder wrapped in tinfoil. Twenty years later his company was selling a $20 Standard Phonograph machine to consumers in the United States and Europe. The era of recorded sound was born.

Over the decades, amateur recording equipment grew in popularity and shrank in size. It wasn't until the 1960s and the mass-marketing of portable cassette-tape machines that home recording became truly commonplace. Still, there are vast riches to be scouted down in recorded sound collections that date back to the 1920s: radio broadcasts, location recordings, newsreels, oral histories, music, speeches, and more. With the growth of online finding aids and websites offering historic films and audio files, the scavenger hunt for recorded sound is getting easier.

Daniel Boorstin writes that historians are limited, quite naturally, by what's available to be discovered. He calls it the "bias of survival." That is, history is not only written about people who leave stuff behind; it is written about people who leave stuff behind that survives. Boorstin's law is true for anyone working with the found objects from the past—documents, images, audio recordings.

Survival bias can have profound implications for the maker of history programs on the radio. If you want to hear history being made, the event needs to have occurred in range of a microphone that happened to be attached to a recording machine that happened to be running at the time. The recorded artifact—phonograph cylinder, spool of steel recording wire, or tape reel—needs to have survived. And it needs to be found. And it needs a working machine on which to play it back. Every one of these prerequisites is an opportunity for the sound to vanish.

In 1994 I made a documentary about a pioneering ethnomusicologist named Frances Densmore. At the turn of the twentieth century she set out for American Indian country with a cylinder phonograph machine to record native music for study and preservation. Most of the field recordings are stored at the Library of Congress's American Folklife Center. The sound survived. But her recordings can be difficult to listen to because a thick haze of surface noise—scratches, clicks, and pops—often obscures the source audio. Yet the cylinder recordings are amazing artifacts of what many feared was a disappearing indigenous musical culture.

Though I had scores of recordings to work with there was virtually nothing of Densmore herself—just the occasional introduction to a singer. The cylinders only lasted about three minutes. If she made test recordings of her own voice I never found them. So I hired an actress to read from Densmore's writings. In one scene she described working among the Sioux in 1911 and asking the old men to describe the sacred Sun Dance, which the U.S. government had banned three decades earlier. Behind this narration I mixed the sound of a buckboard wagon and a team of horses I'd recorded on a farm in Wisconsin. I also had the sound of crickets from a patch of prairie and, mixed low, the call of a meadowlark.

DENSMORE: One afternoon, the entire party drove across the prairie. They scanned the horizon, measuring the distance to the Missouri River and the buttes. At last they gave the signal for the wagons to stop, and began to search. In a short time they found the exact spot where the ceremony was held. The scars were still on their bodies. Some of the Indians put on their war bonnets and their jackets of deerskin with the long fringes. One old man said with trembling lips: "I was young then. My wife and children were with me. They went away many years ago. I wish I could have gone with them."

This slice of history had contemporary meaning. Some native people were using Densmore's recordings and research to more fully reclaim tribal traditions. So to me this is "living history," because we can hear the past— the Indians' voices and their music—and because what happened before still matters.

The programs and pieces I've produced concentrate on particular stories or themes. I doubt I would ever attempt the kind of sweeping historical survey that BBC Radio presented in *This Sceptred Isle*—a comprehensive history of Britain from the Roman invasion to the twentieth century (too bad there's no archival tape from the battle at Waterloo). My projects tend to focus on alternative (or hidden) versions of American history—stories that deepen and complicate that history. In one sense, Frances Densmore represents the kind of iconoclastic, entrepreneurial spirit we often find heroic in frontier characters. But she also argued for the serious study of Indian cultures, which many Americans dismissed as primitive and irrelevant. From our contemporary perspective, Densmore did invaluable work documenting and preserving indigenous cultural lifeways. But she could also be an intrusive and insensitive figure. Some Native Americans have used Densmore's recordings and research to more fully reclaim tribal traditions, while others have complained that she collected sacred songs not meant for outsiders, and that she exploited some of the singers she recorded.

The twenty-minute documentary "Song Catcher, Frances Densmore of Red Wing" aired on NPR's *All Things Considered*. While it can be difficult to get airtime for a story of this length, there's a vital need for good history reporting on the radio. Too many news reports, interview programs, first-person stories, and cultural programs fail to offer a robust explanation of why things happen the way they do. Sometimes, facts are dumped in a heap at the listener's feet like a basket of laundry. Here, you sort it out. All too frequently the background of a story—the historical context—is left out all together, cut for time, or tagged-on deep in the last gasping minutes of a radio piece, especially a news story. But knowledge of the past is critical to making sense of the unfolding present. Radio is especially well suited to telling the quieter, less well-known stories behind historical events—stories that complicate our understanding of what we think we know.

I was prompted by the broadcast of Ken Burns's *The War* on PBS to produce a radio program that looked at World War II from a less monumental perspective. "Battles of Belief" documented the experience of thirty-six conscientious objectors (COs) who chose to serve their country by starving. They were part of a nutrition experiment at the University of Minnesota. The study had two aims: to document the effects of starvation on the body and mind and to discover the best way to feed survivors of famine. The U.S. military hoped to learn how to feed the hungry people who would be liberated from Nazi-controlled Europe. Conscientious objectors were recruited for the experiment.

In World War II, the draft law allowed COs to opt for noncombat service in uniform. Many became medics or worked for a new outfit called the Civilian Public Service. CPS men cleared forest trails, worked on farms, tended patients in mental hospitals, and took part in medical experiments. For "Battles of Belief," a colleague and I interviewed a half-dozen men who had volunteered for the experiment.

JAY GARNER: We were willing to put ourselves on the line to protect other humans. It was the killing that we objected to.

NARRATOR: Jay Garner of Ohio was in the Civilian Public Service. The son of Brethren missionaries, he'd grown up in India and been deeply influenced by the nonviolent teachings of Mahatma Gandhi. Garner had hoped to serve as a combat ambulance driver, but that option was blocked to men in the Civilian Public Service.

GARNER: Soon after I was drafted, I was transferred to the Oregon coast where I was firefighting. Then from there, I transferred to the Augusta state mental hospital taking care of a twenty-bed dormitory of old men, when a brochure came out and said, "Would you starve that others might be better fed?"

HENRY SCHOLBERG: American boys were dying on the battlefields, suffering imprisonment, getting wounded. And I felt it was unfair for me to be able to sleep in a comfortable bed at night and always have three meals. I felt I should be prepared to sacrifice.

Looking back at World War II, it's easy to believe that Americans all felt the same—that fascism was evil and had to be defeated at any cost. We now call it the "Good War," and the people who fought in it the "Greatest Generation." But the story is more complicated and nuanced than that. From its earliest days, World War II was a struggle for minds and hearts, around the world and in the United States. "Battles of Belief" was not intended as a response or a companion to the Ken Burns film, but it used an opportunity—public and media attention to the series—to look at a fascinating and little-known story in American history that helps stretch our national understanding of the war.

The idea for a program on conscientious objectors came from a set of oral history interviews a colleague conducted with some of these men. Oral history collections can be a great asset to radio producers. It's far easier for listeners to care about characters who speak for themselves.

The rise of oral history as an academic practice occurred in the mid-twentieth century. It was championed by such historians as Allan Nevins at Columbia University, who wanted to make "a systematic attempt to obtain from the lips and papers of Americans who had lived significant lives, a fuller record of their accomplishments." Nevins founded Columbia's Oral History Research Office in 1948. With eight thousand taped memoirs, it is the granddaddy of oral history collections in this country. In the 1960s and 70s, oral historians widened the definition of "significant lives" and ac-complishments by increasingly collecting records of the experiences of everyday people.

On the face of it, an oral history archive might seem like a radio pro-ducer's gold mine—swing a pickaxe anywhere and strike riches. It's rarely so easy. Many excellent oral history projects are set up to be *text-centric*. The taped interviews are often meant to produce typed transcripts rather than be used as artifacts themselves. This was especially true in the early years at Columbia, when many tapes got recycled after the transcripts were finished.

In 2001 I produced a documentary called "Remembering Jim Crow" based on a remarkable oral history project begun in the late 1980s by Duke University historians and the Center for Documentary Studies. I came across the collection by accident while doing related research and figured there might be a radio program in there somewhere. There was, but many of the challenges I faced in mining that archive were typical of oral history projects. The collection was well organized but only about a quarter of more than a thousand interviews had been transcribed, and poor tape qual-ity was a major obstacle. The intrepid students who had fanned out across the South to conduct interviews in living rooms and on front porches often perched their microphones far away from the informant. Great stories drowned in the background roar of air conditioners or TV programs. Radio producers are trained to keep quiet when a source is spinning a good yarn. Oral history interviews are often laced with "uh huhs," "okays," and other verbal debris that clutter the sound of the narrative.

Tape that glitters to a radio producer may be dull as dross to the academic specialist and vice versa. Simple questions that could serve a radio audience well may not have been asked. For example, I scrutinized more than two hundred of the Duke University interviews about the segregation era but could not find tape to help explain the peculiar term widely used as a kind of nickname for the period: Jim Crow. No one asked, "Who *was* Jim Crow anyway?" I would like to have heard what people who endured Jim Crow knew or thought of the term.

Much has changed in the practice of oral history in recent years. Practitioners are using better equipment and more effective recording techniques. The increasingly multimedia nature of education and teaching has helped bring about this change. The Oral History Association has also invited radio producers to its national meetings to explore how the two disciplines can benefit one another. Collaborations between oral historians and radio producers have tremendous potential.

In 2002 American RadioWorks teamed up with Gerald Early, professor of English and African American studies at Washington University in St. Louis, to conduct oral history interviews with African American veterans of the Korean War. Nearly a hundred men across the country were interviewed in their homes or at reunions. The interviews were also used in the American RadioWorks documentary "Korea: The Unfinished War," which marked the fiftieth anniversary of the end of the conflict. The tapes were transcribed and posted—in both text and audio form—on a searchable online database and were archived at Washington University.

History is an ever-changing narrative. As each new batch of White House tapes gets released by the National Archives, this extraordinary trove of insider evidence provokes new interpretations of Presidents Kennedy, Johnson, and Nixon. Likewise, the growing collections of oral history interviews covering the Jim Crow era yield new insights into that period of America's past. It's worth noting that these voices were kept silent at the time.

The novelist Milan Kundera wrote, "The struggle of man against power is the struggle of memory against forgetting." I'd add that silence is forgetting's co-conspirator. History on the radio is a powerful ally to memory because the medium works best when we broadcast the kind of lost or obscured voices, the kind of character-driven and emotionally rich stories, that plant ideas and facts more deeply in memory. And, hopefully, beyond the act of remembering lies understanding. As a radio producer I see that as my optimistic destination. America's contemporary racial dilemmas are far better understood when we remember the laws and customs erected during the Jim Crow segregation era. Complex characters from our collective past, like Richard Nixon, become more vivid and perhaps more comprehensible when we hear them in intimate moments, when they *speak* to us.

Sound is a time machine. Hearing history transports us to the past in a powerful, imaginative way. The voices of the past, in all their nuance and texture, pour into our cars and our kitchens. These voices have the power to alter the stories we tell about ourselves, and to change us.

The Voice and the Place

Sandy Tolan

IN THE SUMMER OF 1982, wide-eyed and pumped with a post-Watergate journalistic fervor, I climbed into a borrowed, beat-up Datsun and headed north out of Flagstaff, Arizona, into Navajo country.

I was drawn there by two stories that astounded me both in their intensity and their near invisibility to people outside the reservation. One was about the Navajo uranium miners—foot soldiers of the Cold War and the U.S. atomic weapons program, who had worked in the unventilated "dog holes" across the reservation, chipping at rock and breathing in radioactive dust. Now many of these men, who had never been told of the dangers or even been given protective masks or clothing, were getting sick and dying. A wave of cancer and silicosis had swept through the uranium belt of Navajo country, leaving whole communities nearly empty of men of a certain age. It was astonishing to me. As I write this decades later, I'm still outraged that my own government could have overseen such violent neglect.

The other story was about a group of Navajo resisters, mostly old women armed with shotguns in a place called Big Mountain. These were some of the most traditional people in North America, shepherds dwelling in old mud and log hogans in a high desert country dotted with cedar and sage. In the wake of a long-brewing dispute with the Hopi tribal government, the United States had concocted a plan to relocate the Big Mountain people, and thousands of other Navajos, into suburban-style tract homes in border towns like Winslow and Holbrook. But the old ladies, leaders of the resistance, wouldn't budge.

All that summer and into the fall, I rattled down broken reservation roads, driving through Arizona's pounding monsoon rains and more than once nearly sliding into ditches. It was scary and exhilarating, and not just for the unfamiliar terrain. I was twenty-six years old, driven by a passion for "the people's right to know," and by a simple truth that would be a measure for countless future projects: the stories had gotten under my skin. Armed with my first-ever assignment, from the old NPR *Journal*, I set about producing my first radio documentary.

I had little idea what I was doing. I hardly even knew what a documentary was, much less how to produce one, and the end result—rambling and text-heavy, infused with statistics and self-conscious prose that crowded out eloquent voices—was forgettable. Worth remembering, though, is what I learned from my choppy maiden voyage. The story is in the voice and the place. It was not enough, I found, to merely document hidden realities.

In the following years, first along the U.S.-Mexico border, later in Central and South America, the Balkans, South Asia, the Middle East, and the United States, I would come to understand what I failed to grasp in those early months crisscrossing Navajoland: that the documentary functions best when it is not merely a long piece of fact-jammed journalism but a nonfiction drama set on an audio stage with scenes, characters, narrative arc, dramatic tension, and even silence. Above all it is the characters—the voices—that convey the deepest emotional truth in our medium. Cultivating them, even just identifying them, ranks among the biggest challenges of the radio documentary maker. Nowhere is this more important than in the early stages of production, when I often feel more like a casting director than a journalist.

IN THE WINTER OF 1998 in Los Tapiros, a Mexican shantytown a mile south of the U.S. line in the city of Nogales, Sonora, stood great hulking American factories that were part of the maquiladora industry. American companies would ship boxes of parts into Mexico; workers would assemble the parts into products—file folders, false teeth, blue jeans, televisions—for export back into the United States. Alongside the assembly plants were the shacks workers had built from the cardboard boxes and wooden pallets that had carried parts across the border. It was Dickens's London on the border—the story of two great migrations, one of American and multinational companies heading south in search of cheap labor and lax environmental and safety laws, and the other of poor young Mexicans traveling north to seek work. On a January morning my collaborator, Jerry

Kammer, and I walked through Los Tapiros, which was literally built in the shadow of a gray cinderblock factory that cranked out garage-door openers for sale in Sears stores north of the line. As we took in the scene we realized that we couldn't simply describe the place, its history, and the economic and political reasons thousands of such factories were sprouting up all along the border. We needed to tell the big story through a smaller one, and for that we needed to begin casting our main characters. We wanted to tell the story through one Mexican family.

But this wasn't going to be so easy. First, we had to get beyond the understandable reserve of workers who wondered why two white American guys were so interested in the details of their lives. Then, for those who invited us to sit and chat—on rickety plastic chairs or overturned milk crates, sipping hot coffee and eating huge, tasty Sonoran-style tortillas—there was the challenge of figuring out how representative a family was. Had they come from the south, as most migrants did? Were they working in various factories, which would allow us to explore the range of work through individuals? Did anyone happen to have a green card and go back and forth to work in Arizona, as was often the case? In other words, would we be able to explain the *whole* by exploring the *particular*?

Then, once we had identified such a family, how open would they be? Were there good storytellers in the family? I had already learned that we journalists, especially documentary makers, are biased against the inarticulate. We had to find good talkers.

And even if all those concerns were resolved, was there any family who would really allow us to hang out with them, sometimes day and night, or follow them in the predawn moments from the family home to join the flow of workers pouring through the factory gate?

It took weeks until we finally found such a family—the Martinezes of Navojoa, Sonora, which was three hundred miles south of Nogales. The family's *Grapes of Wrath* journey bespoke the push of devastated farmlands in the south and the pull of low-wage work in the north. And their determination and dignity amid harsh circumstances was representative of many Mexican migrant families: they managed to emerge from their dirt-floor shacks, which were devoid of electric light or running water, as crisp and shining as any American family across the border in Arizona. Martina

Martinez went to work in the Nogales garage-door opener factory. Her big sister, Maria Luisa, sewed brassieres in the Sara Lee plant. Bety assembled sunglasses at the Foster Grant factory; a cousin built carburetors. Pancho, the oldest brother, had a green card and was looking for better-paying work in the vegetable-packing plants north of the line. The voices of the Martinezes first reached public radio listeners through *Soundprint*, and then later on *All Things Considered*.

By the early 1990s, when my partners in Homelands Productions embarked on the seven-hour documentary series *Vanishing Homelands* for NPR, casting had become a regular part of our work. We used it to evoke the slavelike conditions of Haitian sugarcane cutters in the Dominican Republic; the urban migration of former Honduran corn farmers to Tegucigalpa; and the colonization of the frontier along the Pan American Highway.

Never have I spent more time or effort in casting than in the Middle East, where in 1998, I sought out a story that would probe the human side of the Israeli-Palestinian conflict. Despite the forests of newspaper stories and miles of videotape documenting the bloody repetition of war and violence, there had been precious little reporting that linked the histories of the two peoples in tangible ways, that traced the shared ground of enemies. I spent weeks reading Israeli military history, Palestinian oral histories, and scholarly treatises to learn as much as I could about the roots of the conflict. I traveled from Jerusalem to Tel Aviv, from Ramallah to Hebron to Gaza, to find the human story that would move beyond the heartbreaking images transmitted from the region. I encountered many dead ends and broken leads, but then I came across something real: the true story of one house and two families who shared a common history. A history that emanated from the walls of a house made of Jerusalem stone on the coastal plain east of Tel Aviv and Jaffa. *The Lemon Tree*, a documentary made for *Fresh Air*, became the seed for the book of the same name. And perhaps more than ever, it was the power of the human voice—in this case, the voices of Israeli Dalia Eshkenazi Landau and Palestinian Bashir al-Khairi —that conveyed the emotional truth of longing, love, and conflict.

BASHIR: We were walking toward my house. I was confronting the unknown, lost in thought. How was I going to be received in that house? Who was going to be behind these closed doors in my home?

DALIA: That day I was on a summer vacation from the university. Alone at home, my parents were working.

BASHIR: Should I knock forcefully and risk intimidating the people inside, or knock softly and risk that the people would not hear me? I found the bell. I pressed the bell.

DALIA: And the doorbell of the big gate rang,

BASHIR: I was taking everything in. I looked at the walls of the house, the windows, the trees. I saw the flowering tree; it has a beautiful scent. And the towering palm tree, taller than the house. And I saw the lemon tree. [Pause.] After a few seconds, I heard a voice in Hebrew, saying, "*Kyen, kyen*" which means, "Yes?"

DALIA: When I opened I saw these three men with suits and ties, in the summer, July, in Israel. [Laughs.]

BASHIR: The door opened and I found myself face to face with a young woman in her twenties.

DALIA: They were very wary and very shy, and they didn't know how they would be received. But it was like in a split second; it was as if I was always waiting for them.

BASHIR: I told her, I'm the son of the man who owned the house, who lived here before 1948. And I lived here, too.

DALIA: I knew at that moment that it was like completing a puzzle. It was like the second part of an unfinished reality was there, confronting me.

[a beat of silence; piano music comes up subtly]

BASHIR: And I said, is it possible for me to come in and see the house?

[beat; piano]

DALIA: And I opened the door wide, and I said yes, to come in.

[fade up piano music to full; hold for seven seconds]

Sometimes the main "character" is not a person but a place, brought to life by "scene building": weaving voices with strong, succinct description and telling use of sound.

For a documentary about the devastation of indigenous lands in the Ecuadoran Amazon, I built one scene by starting with the mournful sound of a man calling for a canoe to get him across a river, followed by the layered sounds of a small motorboat, the slapping of the bow on the waves, the landing of the boat on the far shore, the sound of crickets and barking dogs in the village, and finally the voice of Toribe, a young indigenous leader. All this was interlaced with my description, which ultimately brought listeners into the young man's home. There he lay in his hammock "staring up at a ceiling of warped gray boards." I described "the dark image of his hands dancing along the far wall, projected by a flicker from the kerosene lamp. He shakes his head, remembering." Then above a symphony of crickets, Toribe says:

> The changes have been so fast—one on top of the other. Our forefathers lived miraculous lives. We hunted in peace, wherever we wanted to go. We worked our fields. We lived from the natural medicines. Now, almost all that is gone.

UP TO NOW I'VE CITED documentaries driven by a journalistic agenda, with characters, places, and scenes put to use in the service of a broader story about an issue or policy. But every now and then I'll encounter a story that is so overpowering in its own right, I don't ask myself whether it represents anything larger in society. Sometimes, the story just wants to tell itself.

In the mid-1990s, I got a chilling email from my old friend Debra Gwartney in Oregon. She wrote that her two eldest daughters, then ages thirteen and fifteen, had run away from home and had been missing for months. In the year that followed I would learn of Debra's harrowing search for her children among anarchist kids in the streets of Eugene and among drugged-out homeless people in San Francisco's Tenderloin district. Eventually, after a year-long odyssey they were lucky to survive, the girls came home. As mother and daughters tried to stitch their lives together, they agreed to let me interview them, independently and at length on and off for more than a year, about what had happened, and why. *Runaway* was originally broadcast on *This American Life* in 2002. Like *The Lemon Tree*, the piece depended almost entirely on the voices telling the story—in this case, of Debra and her daughters, Amanda and Stephanie. I wrote no script and used no natural sound, but simply scored it, at Debra's suggestion, with cello music by David Darling and Yo-Yo Ma. (In early 2009, Debra's own story of those years, *Live through This: A Mother's Memoir of Runaway Daughters and Reclaimed Love*, was published by Houghton Mifflin.)

DEBRA: The next couple of months, every now and then, Amanda would call—never Stephanie—and either leave a message or she'd get me on the phone and say, "We're alive, we're okay." But she'd never tell me where they were. And I would say, "Come home. You need to come home, we need to work this out." She'd just hang up.

STEPHANIE: When we were in San Francisco, that was the crazy times. Me and Amanda, that's where we first started doing dope. . . . [She describes a night in the Tenderloin district, during a period where she was temporarily separated from Amanda. High on alcohol and pills, she was assaulted by a knife-wielding crackhead.]

I remember walking, and just being covered with blood. And I walked up to Sixth and Market and all my friends are sitting there. . . . My mouth is open and there's blood everywhere. And my friend cleaned it up for me. [Pause.] It felt like there was almost a protection around us, or a bubble. Just something protecting Amanda and I. Something special about our journey through this dark place. We just glided through it and remained untouched.

AMANDA: She and I have such a different way of looking at that time. She was so happy, and she felt like she was making this part in this community. I felt used. My idea of the whole thing was to put my life on my back and just go. And stop looking back, stop feeling guilty, stop all these raging emotions. Just keep going, keep moving. I had saved about $1,500 and I had an ATM card. And so we would panhandle and we would live off what I had. Until I got a heroin habit, and then it went pretty fast.

All these stories—from Navajo country to Jerusalem, from the Ecuadoran Amazon to the Oregon coast—share a common terrain. Each is a story I felt I had to tell. They all passed the "under my skin" test: telling the story became a personal imperative. That imperative forced me to find ways financially to make the documentary—by accepting lean times in the early years and, later, by broadening my financial base. The Navajo story, for example, was fueled by my youthful willingness to get by on a cheeseburger and a tank of gas; in later years grant money and income from teaching, which I love, helped me stay on the story. The generosity of the Corporation for Public Broadcasting and other foundations has allowed me and my partners in Homelands Productions (Jonathan Miller, Alan Weisman, and Cecilia Vaisman) the luxury of doing the time-intensive *documentation* that makes a long-form documentary possible.

Often, however, money is scarce and insufficient for lengthy field work, or the circumstances dictate quick action based on instinct and the available time. Some of the best documentary subjects are the ones grabbed quickly, in a snap judgment, before they slip away forever. In the fall of 2007, on a cold morning along the Kosovo-Albania border, I had all of fifteen minutes to get to the heart of the story. My assignment, from *Marketplace* for our Homelands series WORKING, was to find a story about a team of "deminers" clearing land mines along the border. Each of the WORKING stories was focused on a single person's labors, and here I was searching for that one guy who worked at the edge of the land mine zone. As the workers stood around a fire pit on their lunch break, I had a quarter of an hour to interview the group to determine which man had the requisite openness, eloquence, and experience to describe his work and how he saw the world around him.

As the men munched cheese sandwiches and roasted sausages, I asked them questions about the tragedy in the Balkans and how their work to remove land mines might help life here return to normal. Some spoke with bravado; others complained about low wages; one glowered and said not a thing. (*Not that guy*, I thought.) But one man, Valdet Dule (pronounced *doo*-lay), spoke with ease, thoughtfulness, and humor. Above all, it was his body language that made it clear this was my guy. He was sitting cross-legged while leaning against a friend, and he seemed completely at ease, even though his job was among the most dangerous in the world. I approached Valdet after the lunch break. Could we (photographer Dana Wilson and I) follow him around for a couple of days? *Sure*, he said. Including going back to his house in Kosovo? *Of course!* Could we even spend the night at his house, to get the flavor of his family life? *Well . . . why not?* And that was it—from this high-pressure "flash-casting" came our story, which we reported in two days.

The story was for *Marketplace*, where an eight-minute piece is considered *really long*. So the bigger question is, even when there is money to underwrite the time required to find the great characters, scenes, and stories, who puts long-form work on the air? In 1992 and 1993, most of our nearly two dozen *Vanishing Homelands* pieces aired on NPR at seventeen minutes or longer. Many were twenty-two-minute-long "format breakers" for *All Things Considered* (ATC). Now, it's hard to get a piece longer than six minutes on ATC or *Morning Edition*, and the consequences for long-form storytelling are real. Shorter formats mean fewer scenes, less use of telling or "metaphorical" sound, not as much character development, and therefore less nuance and complexity. This is not to say that documentary-style work is impossible in such formats; rich, tightly layered jewels such as The Kitchen Sisters' *Hidden Kitchens* series, for example, still find a home on NPR's big-audience shows. And the *Radio Diaries* format-breakers for ATC are another exception that proves the rule.

But most producers have long since realized that they need to find another place to play their long-form work. Happily, a lot of options have sprung up since the days when *All Things Considered*, like Ma Bell before the breakup, served as the central launching point for so much of America's documentary work. Over the years as format crunch has gripped the network—just like the rest of America's news culture—little radio Sprints and Verizons have sprung up. Smaller, feistier, and more open than the big shows, they have names like *Radio Lab*, *Hearing Voices*, *This American Life*, and *American RadioWorks*. These shows have smaller audiences than the drive-time juggernauts; they air at night or on weekends, and on fewer stations, but encourage new and long-form ways of telling stories. Then there's the "content depot" of the Public Radio Exchange (PRX), where producers post their documentaries online to an audience that includes programmers for local public radio stations. Stations that broadcast a piece then pay a fee to the producer, through PRX. The process bypasses network gatekeepers entirely. The ultimate in audio self-publishing though is the podcast, where a producer's work can compete for new ears along with countless thousands of other websites. A precious few producers might even make a living this way.

Taken together, these outlets are not simply examples of new homes for documentary makers; rather, they exist in part because of the storyteller's burning wish to chronicle the truth as he or she sees it, *and* because of an audience that still hungers to hear long-form nonfiction. This is why documentaries will never go away. Despite the challenges of money and time, there will always be storytellers—people for whom the story creeps under their skin, people who are driven to reveal a hidden truth in the spirit of the people's right to know. And always, despite the crunching formats and splintering distribution, there will be people who want to listen and who will find their way to the work.

Crossing Borders

Maria Martin

MY MOTHER WAS ADELA GARCIA RÍOS, whose family came from the indigenous community of Texcoco and who worked as household help in Mexico City. My father, Charles McGlynn Martin, was a *gringo* escapee from a cold climate. He'd ventured south from Chicago after World War II to find sun and cheap living on the GI Bill. The son of Irish immigrants and the Mexico City gal together forged *una familia bilingüe y bicultural*—a bilingual, bicultural family—symbolic of the many connections between the United States and its southerly neighbor.

We lived in Mexico for my first six years; I spent the next six years of my life along the border in Arizona and Texas. When I was twelve, we moved to California. I start with this story of my beginnings because I don't think I would have the sensibilities and perspectives of the observer, the "outsider," the journalist, had it not been for living in two countries and being the child of a bicultural marriage. In many ways, the borders I've crossed all my life, and the bridges of cross-cultural understanding I've attempted to create through radio, all began right in my family.

In the 1970s, when I discovered radio (or, rather, radio discovered me), being a journalist was the farthest thing from my mind. There were few role models in the media to encourage a Latina, even a bicultural Latina like myself, to aspire to a career on TV or on the radio. At least, I was not aware of any.

In my early years at school along the border, we were punished for speaking Spanish. But things were beginning to change in the late sixties and early seventies, as the African American civil rights movement inspired another movement for cultural and political affirmation among Mexican Americans and other Latinos. As a university student, I'd changed my major from political science to Chicano studies. I joined a Chicana student group, Mujeres por la Raza.

One day in the mid-70s, in the wine country of northern California, I was absent-mindedly turning the radio dial when I heard something I'd never, *ever* heard before: it was in English *and* in Spanish. The station played reggae, rancheras, and *dedicas* (dedications) on the oldies show, and covered public affairs. For the first time in my life, I heard media that reflected my reality as a bilingual and bicultural person of Mexican *and* American heritage. What I was listening to were the sounds of the very early days of KBBF 89.1 on the FM dial in Santa Rosa, California—the first Latino-operated and -owned public radio station. As Oprah would say, it was an "Aha Moment" —I was hooked on this pioneering little radio station and on making radio that cut across cultural lines.

In a few weeks, I wasn't just a listener of 89.1's "bilingual broadcasting," I was a volunteer producer for *Somos Chicanas*, a weekly talk show addressing Hispanic women's issues—probably the first radio program of its kind. Consequently, it was somewhat controversial. Birth control, women's sexuality, and abortion were among its topics. Women—especially Latinas, and particularly low-income farm-working women—had *never* had the media address them directly. When they called in, they'd tell us they'd had to leave home to use the corner pay phone—God forbid their husbands should overhear them calling in to this *programa sin vergüenza*—this "shameless" radio program. I was then (and thirty-some years later still remain) amazed by the power of radio to touch people's lives and make them take action.

One night in particular stands out in my memory: I was on the air after the *Somos Chicanas* program, hosting a music show. The phone rang, and at first all I could hear were sobs. In Spanish mixed with tears, a woman told me she was calling from the hospital. She'd taken an overdose of pills, but she wailed, no one at the hospital could understand her (in those days before bilingual ATMs and health workers).

The woman had turned to the one thing in this country she trusted— her radio station. This constant source of news and information spoke to her in her language, played her music, and was, above all, her lifeline. Again, then as now, I was enthralled by the power of the microphone, the power of radio.

I think about that night often as I look back at how and why media—the kind I've done, the kind that hopefully has served to connect people— became my life. Because of my parents, my background, I've always felt deeply the need to bridge languages and cultures. Maybe I felt so strongly about KBBF and the power of media to build bridges of cultural understanding because, like that woman who called me in tears one night so long ago, I also needed a lifeline—one that would bring together my two worlds, my two Americas, with compassion and understanding.

MY WORK IS ROOTED in the recommendations of the long-ago Hutchins Commission. Officially known as the Commission on Freedom of the Press, it outlined in 1947 the responsibilities of the news media in a democratic society, stating that the press had the obligation to project a "representative picture of the constituent groups in the society." I believe this is at the core of a responsible press—that part of telling the truth is to reflect the society in all its many voices.

When I was at the University of Portland in the late 1960s, just a few years before discovering my radio destiny, I remember studying another commission's report. President Lyndon Johnson had created the Kerner Commission (formally, the National Advisory Commission on Civil Disorders) to examine the causes of the race riots that had erupted across the country. The commission's conclusion was that the media's inaccurate portrayals and misrepresentations of the African American community contributed to racial divisions in our nation.

In that then black and white America (as it was perceived), both the Hutchins and the Kerner Commissions urged the media to improve their coverage of minority issues. I firmly believe these recommendations are as valid today as they were when they were issued—and even more so as American society moves beyond black and white, as global reality dictates that we can no longer afford not to understand the "other."

According to the U.S. Census Bureau, by the year 2050 nearly 25 percent of the population will be Latino. As our country undergoes this dramatic demographic shift, it's clear to me that media—and public broadcasting in particular—have a distinct social responsibility to provide that "representative portrayal of society's constituent groups" that the Hutchins Commission called for decades ago. While I admire the work of those who produce the artful documentary, I perceive a greater need for radio to play a substantive role in bridging cultures and creating understanding through fair, accurate, and inclusive information.

This was the reason I left National Public Radio to start the program *Latino USA* in the early 1990s. As an editor on the network's National Desk, it was frustratingly apparent that even some of my very talented and educated colleagues lacked an understanding of the complexities of the Latino experience. Often, when Latino issues were even considered, the focus was on viewing Hispanics as "problem people"—that is, with the emphasis on stories about gangs and undocumented immigration. I wanted to create a radio vehicle that would portray the whole of the Latino experience, its complexity and diversity, its beauty and its pain. I wanted to hear the voices of Latino intellectuals, as well as people on the street, speaking English and Spanish and all the combinations in between, which gives such vibrancy and texture to Hispanic communities from Miami to Alaska. I wanted a radio program that would allow the key audiences that listen to public radio to know that Latinos are not a monolithic group. I wanted to have a place on public radio for Latinos to feel at home—where Puerto Ricans could learn about Mexican Americans and Cubans about Dominicans and Central Americans and vice versa.

The kind of radio I produce is not only about mission but also about craft. It's not enough to produce programs that people "should" listen to. On the contrary, I hope the "reality radio" I make is something audiences want to hear. If making radio that touches people's hearts and minds has been one of my guiding production values over the last three decades, the other is "hook them in!" I make every attempt to win over listeners with compelling sound, inspired pacing, vivid writing, and informed editing.

The sounds of the communities I cover often motivate and guide creative production. Music, cadences of speech, the different accents of my subjects (whether speaking English, Spanish, or an indigenous idiom) can all add another dimension to a story, a new layer of richness to a production.

Voice-over translations pose an opportunity for creating lovely sound montages, with one language weaving in and out of the other. In addition, how one treats voice-overs and uses original interviews can serve to validate (or not) the humanity of one's subjects.

For instance, when I'm working with a Spanish-language interview, I strive to establish what a person is saying first—let him or her express a complete thought before bringing in the English-language voice-over. To establish a complete thought may sometimes take ten or twelve seconds—perhaps even longer—but in that process one validates the dignity of the person whose voice is part of the production and whose story I'm telling. By allowing non-English language to breathe, we also show respect for the increasing number of Americans who speak Spanish and other languages, and who—more and more each day—are becoming part of our audience.

I also find that in order to keep the production interesting, I'll sometimes alternate between voice-overs and paraphrases, even in the same interview.

I used all of these techniques in the twelve-part series *Después de las Guerras: Central America after the Wars*, which aired in 2004 and 2005. One segment explores the issue of indigenous identity—a main character is a fifteen-year-old young Mayan woman named Casimira Xiloj Herrera who has made the decision to break away from her mother's and grandmother's tradition of wearing indigenous clothing, called *traje*. In one scene, I created a trilingual production—as Casimira speaks to her Quiché Maya-speaking grandmother through her mother, who translates from Spanish to Quiché Maya.

In another piece from the series, "Santa Maria: A Tale of One Village," I used voice-overs for a massacre survivor, Edwin, and his father, Manuel Canil. Edwin's story is so poignant and powerful that I attempted to weave the two languages together in such a way as to have much of the original version heard in the clear—I think the authentic emotion comes through even for those who don't speak Spanish. At the same time, the voice that translates Edwin's story has a powerful quality of its own, which I believe enhances the entire scene. Here's the transcript from that segment:

EDWIN: *Hay veces que se me dificulta, pero si hay veces que si puedo* . . . [Edwin's voice fades for my paraphrase.]

NARRATION: Edwin Canil says it's hard for him to talk about the events of February 1982. . . . In the United States then, Ronald Reagan was president. . . . The headlines in U.S. newspapers told of other happenings in Central America, in El Salvador and Nicaragua, but there was little news of what was taking place in this part of the region—about how, just south of the Mexican border, a column of Guatemalan soldiers marched into the isolated jungle settlement called Santa María Tzejá. Edwin was just six years old then . . .

EDWIN: [We hear Edwin telling his story, as the Spanish rolls untranslated for fifteen seconds.] *Solo recuerdo que salí corriendo me metí entre la vegetación. . . . El ejército con toda su carga, y yo no puedo pasar entre eso . . . y* [sighs] *. . . y no me fui muy lejos. . . .* [Spanish fades, voice-over comes in]

ENGLISH VOICE-OVER: I only remember running. . . . When I heard the gun shots and screams, I didn't turn around [Spanish very audible under this]. . . . There was a fallen tree trunk, and there I hid. Then I heard a little girl crying, and it was my little sister. . . . It seemed as if I were watching a play. Then, I saw a soldier lift her up and take out his knife . . . and . . . [pause]

EDWIN: [voice comes up] *. . . y cuando vi un soldado . . . agarró y levantó a mi hermanita . . . sacó su cuchillo . . .* [Edwin becomes more emotional, he pauses, chokes up. We hear this for six to seven seconds.]

ENGLISH VOICE-OVER CONTINUES: He took her arm and cut it off, and threw it away. . . . I did not understand what I was seeing, I did not know what death was [long pause]. Later, when the soldiers left [sobs in background], I went back to where the bodies lay in a circle, and I laid down with them, waiting for them to wake up—my mother, my grandmother, my cousins and uncles . . . my little sister. . . . I began to talk to them: "Mother. Grandmother." They wouldn't answer, they wouldn't wake up.

EDWIN: [voice comes up] *. . . nadie se levanta, nadie . . . y vi a mi hermanita—lo que yo recuerdo. Vi a mi hermanita, ya no tenía cabeza, se despedazó todo . . .*

ENGLISH VOICE-OVER: Then I saw my little sister, without her head. . . . My mother, with a bullet. . . . I was afraid, I was scared. Then I left. . . . [sniffs]

EDWIN: [voice comes up] *. . . fue la primera vez que sentí miedo, y salí . . .*

I "auditioned" various voices for the role of Edwin. For the voice of the father, the amazing survivor Manuel Canil, I knew that the voice of the maestro and Xic-Indio (Chicano/Indian) poet Raul Salinas would not only be great for radio but would also reflect the spirit of Manuel—two voices from different continents with somewhat related life experiences, coming together through radio documentary production to tell a powerful tale.

IT'S ALWAYS BEEN CLEAR to me that one cannot tell the Latino story without creating an understanding of the links that bind U.S. Hispanics and their Latin American homelands . . . or for that matter, the historical, social, and economic links that bind the countries of this hemisphere to the United States. I've tried to forge these connections with some of the reporting I've done from Latin America—Mexico, Bolivia, and Central America, in particular.

A few years ago, as part of a personal initiative to deepen my connections with journalists in Latin America, I applied for Fulbright and Knight International Press fellowships to work with journalists in Uruguay and Guatemala. The experience changed my life; at the same time, it took me back to the days of bilingual radio KBBF—to a time when it was so apparent that for many communities radio was a lifeline, not a luxury.

It is not surprising, for instance, that some of the first battles for media democratization in Guatemala since the signing of peace accords more than ten years ago are being fought over radio frequencies. Or that in Bolivia and Venezuela governments trying to create social change are setting up community radio networks. While television, cable, and the Internet are making inroads throughout the continent, radio remains the most powerful mass medium in the region, reaching hills and rural areas away from the cities where television cannot.

Radio in places like Guatemala, Bolivia, and Uruguay is truly a people's medium. I was greatly impressed with the journalists I met and worked with—*comunicadores sociales* who possess a strong commitment to serving the public and to helping their listeners become active participants in a peaceful democracy.

They often do this with few resources, and with little protection from the law. Often, they work at risk to their lives and livelihoods. Their experiences reinspired me at a time when I needed to look beyond the politics of public radio and the continued resistance in some quarters to serving a changing audience. I've found myself spending more and more time teaching and working with these *periodistas empíricos* (journalists with no formal training), sharing my experiences and learning from theirs . . . recalling a time when I too had little formal training but a great deal of commitment to telling the stories that would make a difference and, maybe, a little better world.

Adventurers in Sound

Karen Michel

ONE OF THE BETTER PIECES of radio I've heard in many years was made by a blind teenager in a small town in New York's Catskill Mountains. Not that I listened to it on public radio; the story was broadcast locally on a—get this—hydropowered community radio station. I heard it presented in a workshop for teenage radio producers at a conference of the National Federation of Community Broadcasters. The story was about a blind person's experience of learning to drive.

When I met Amanda Martins in that workshop, she didn't introduce herself as blind (though for the sighted, this was obvious) but as a klutz. This self-proclaimed klutz had a skilled dancer's ear for the choreography of radio.

The story begins, "Recently, I got to experience what few blind people have experienced: I drove a car." She continues to tell us that driving has "always been more of a wistful dream than something I thought would actually happen."

INSTRUCTOR: When I yell stop, you stop.
MARTINS, NARRATING: After a few mishaps . . .
PASSENGER/INSTRUCTOR: The horse is in the way!
MARTINS: Can I hit the horse?

There's lots of laughter, even when she almost hits a person. And in case we thought she was doing a good job, Martins reminds us, "Contrary to popular belief, all blind people are not good drivers. For example, while attempting to drive around the track I somehow ended up in a field." We hear her open the door and reach down to feel the tall grass.

"I wasn't the only one having difficulties though," Martins confides as her teacher says, "Wow, this is tough telling someone how to drive."

165

MARTINS, NARRATING: But really I have no complaints and even though I was a little scared, I had a lot of fun.

MARTINS, TO INSTRUCTOR: Did I do OK?

INSTRUCTOR: Yeah, you did fine. I got to have the experience of a lifetime, and despite appearances none of us was in real danger.

Self-effacing and funny, the piece brings us into the experience of the story. And it's a story told from a distinctly teen perspective.

I'm old enough to believe that radio needs new voices, literally, and in the sense of voice as expression of the soul. And so for some years I've worked with teenagers: in rural Alaska, in tiny community stations, in workshops around the country, and at WNYC with their Radio Rookies. I seek to teach them the skills, the means, and the methods for telling stories that I've learned in the hope that they will come up with their own tales and ways of telling them, taking what I've learned if they want it, discarding what keeps them from finding their own voices. Public radio needs people willing to use the medium in new ways, and teenagers are uniquely qualified for this.

Teens, in my experience, primarily tell stories in the first person. Everything relates to them—as they explore what it means to be human, to have responsibilities, to perceive life and become an actor in that life. They are secure in the knowledge that what they have to say matters, that attention should be paid.

That means that it's hard to take big-picture issues and ask a teen to do a radio story in the ingrained style of most NPR-ish features, a style that could be characterized as largely disembodied, as if reporters are merely a pass-through, a conduit—that they, and the Official Experts they include to give "outside perspectives," provide the listener all one needs or should want to know. Teens haven't learned the rules for that kind of radio making. As a result, their work is often startlingly illuminating.

THOUGH I STARTED WORKING with teenagers not long after I started my own so-called radio career—with Koyukon Athabaskan kids in a remote Yukon River village in Alaska—I've never stopped doing my own work. Always, I'm trying to find other ways to tell stories; and I'm always, I hope, open to teens teaching me different ways to hear and see.

One of my best teachers has been Samr "Rocky" Tayeh. He's done several stories for WNYC's Radio Rookies, where I served as the consulting editor for several years. Rocky is best known—in the world of public radio he is famous—for his story about his war with obesity. I've never worked with a person who has his gift for dealing with what is (literally) deadly serious in such a self-deprecating and ultimately insightful way. He was 16, 6'1", and weighed 400 pounds. When he'd stand on the scale, it would read, "Invalid." His parents tried bribing him to lose weight with offers of a computer, a thousand dollars, normalcy. Rocky told us about his truly insatiable appetite; he kept a log of what he ate. Rocky followed up that story with another, about his decision to have lap-band surgery, as he says, to save his life. By the time he was a senior at his Brooklyn, New York, high school he weighed five hundred pounds and needed special desks.

One of the challenges we had while collaborating on his follow-up story was to find a way to clue in listeners who hadn't heard "My Struggle with Obesity" but not repeat too much for those who had. After many attempts to figure out how to do it, he addressed the problem in "Battling Obesity: The Story of Rocky's Reduction."

ROCKY: When I was eleven years old, I made a promise I couldn't keep. I was on vacation at my uncle's house. And after a fun day of swimming—with my shirt on, of course—I went into the bathroom and nervously stepped on the scale: 200 pounds. So I swore to Allah, something you're not supposed to do in the bathroom, that I wouldn't get any fatter. But I could never slam the door on food—my comfort for life, my best friend in chocolate, vanilla, and strawberry.

SISTER: You have a choice to lose weight! Just now you ate a pint of ice cream, is that necessary?

ROCKY: I ate a pint of ice cream.

SISTER: You ate a pint of ice cream, strawberry ice cream!

ROCKY: That's my twin sister and me. I recorded it when I was fifteen for my first radio story.

SISTER: Yesterday you ate three bowls of cereal.

ROCKY: It wasn't strawberry ice cream. It was fudge ice cream.

ROCKY: The night before my story aired I thought everyone was just going to hear me as a fat-sad-complainer who really didn't want to lose weight.

Listeners responded to the first story, and some of those letters appear in Rocky's follow-up.

LETTER 1: This message is for Rocky . . .

ROCKY AS NARRATOR: But so many people wrote in. And I didn't feel alone anymore!

LETTER 2: Isn't it ironic that despite being a Jewish anorexic, I identified with Rocky . . .

LETTER 3: . . . that means having healthy munchies around, you know raisins, fruits.

LETTER 4: If Rocky wants to ask me about it, tell him to feel free to e-mail me or call me.

LETTER 5: Unbelievable.

ROCKY: I went from hiding my problems to telling millions of strangers.

FROM THE *JANE PAULEY SHOW*: Live from 30 Rockefeller Plaza, on the *Jane Pauley Show* . . .

ROCKY: When the *Jane Pauley Show* came knocking I was fatter than ever.

ROCKY [on the show]: My name is Rocky, I am sixteen . . .

ROCKY: There I was, in soft focus . . . with what seemed like my only friends in the world: my cat, Simba, and of course, the refrigerator.

ROCKY [on the show]: I need to lose weight or I am going to die.

Rocky goes on to tell us of his experiences on TV, his appointment with the lap-band doctor, his interfamily squabbling over whether or not to tell his father, and, finally, what it's like post-surgery for a guy whose best friend is the fridge.

ROCKY: But months after surgery I was trying to push the lap band to the limit, first with Pringles, then with Chinese food. My Saturday night dates with TV and food continued. The lap band controlled how much I ate, but it didn't control why I ate. So what do I do when I'm sad, frustrated, or bored? . . .

I feel really full, my body is telling me no, but my mind is telling me, yeah. I have to learn to accept me, or I am just going to keep on throwing up and throwing up. There comes the soup. I definitely ate too much. I'm hovering over the sink because I know it's coming out. Bluuuuh. And there goes my dinner, back into the sink.

That "bluuuuh" is a rough transliteration of the sound of Rocky throwing up, something he did often as a result of eating too much. Rocky decided to keep that indelicate sonic moment but shortened the time it actually took. Even shortened, it makes for incredibly powerful listening, and it leads one to the sobering thought that Rocky, who's struggling to live as a "normal" person, may still be in danger of killing himself. I haven't heard an adult come close to doing a story about childhood or adult obesity in such a direct way. Partly it may be that adults wouldn't want to be known by how much they weigh—it's an aspect worth overlooking. To Rocky, his weight is worth examining. He has something to tell us, the listeners, from his own experience.

WORKING WITH TEENS—to find a subject that interests them enough to stick with it for months after school, and to find the focus for their story and execute it—has taught me a lot, about story structure and approach, about allowing for nuance. I've become more flexible in my own work, more willing to visit the "I" along with the "you," the listeners. My radio work and my attitude toward the possibilities of making aural stories have flexed as a result of collaborating with teenagers.

Some years back, post-9/11, there was a public radio initiative; all stations were to collaborate on airing stories about "democracy." A national show (Wisconsin Public Radio's *To the Best of Our Knowledge*) approached me to do a story, and I said sure, so long as I didn't have to mention the "d" word. I was interested in what people lived for, would die for, would kill for. And while out asking these questions, of maybe a hundred people in a thirty-mile radius from my home, people sometimes asked me for my answers. Somehow it had never occurred to me that my opinion mattered. So I did the story starting out with "me," giving my answers, though briefly. More recently, I revisited the project, asking folks those same three little big questions around Durham, North Carolina, where I was living during an academic year at the Center for Documentary Studies. This time, it was very much about me and my reflections on what I saw and heard. Without those years of working with teens, I very much doubt that would have been the case. The intimacy of self-expression would have been replaced by the distance to the "you" out there. I'm much more willing to experiment with the possibilities of sonic storytelling because I've been asking teens to do just that.

Acting as midwife for teen radio stories isn't easy. I like to have the teenagers dictate to me, and I type whatever they say into the computer. They keep journals, too, and audio diaries. Out of these many pages and hours of recorded sound comes the focusing in on a story. Sorting, weeding, and shaping. Limitations and possibilities. Details. What makes a story original. It can be hard to persuade kids that what's immensely absorbing to them may not engage someone else. So much of what makes a story something another person will want to hear is about the reporter paying attention to the other, not the self. Done well, radio is an art form. Technique precedes the art and enhances it.

RADIO IS A WONDERFUL MEDIUM for hearing one's own and others' voices, for the growth that allows teens and the rest of us to share and reflect. Hopefully, some of these teens will reach us through whatever technologies exist, and hopefully, too, there will some day be regular spots on the air for their stories and insights. They will become the adventurers in sound, heading off into that territory that we once claimed as our own. We all know the sound of civilized radio; let's hear it for the teens who can cannibalize the good parts, chew them up, and come up with something new. Attention will be paid.

Dressy Girls

Lena Eckert-Erdheim

I GREW UP WITHOUT A TELEVISION and, for as long as I can remember, was fed steadily on National Public Radio instead. Because of this, I was pretty much the dorkiest kid I knew all the way through middle school. While my classmates progressed through *Barney*, *Pokemon*, and *Friends*, I was rushing to my radio at five o'clock every evening and humming along to the *All Things Considered* theme music. It never occurred to me that I might one day be on the radio until the summer of 2003 while participating in the Youth Document Durham summer program at the Center for Documentary Studies (CDS). That summer we were talking about sex and using writing, photography, and audio to learn about and document as many different subtopics as we could. Contrary to what you might expect from a group of thirteen-, fourteen-, and fifteen-year-olds, we were very serious and spent a good deal of time wrestling with issues like the representation of women in the media and sexual violence. Out of these discussions and a trip to a crisis response center came my first radio pieces about the role— or perceived role—of clothes in cases of sexual assault.

Despite my close to lifelong addiction to listening to the radio, it took me a while to warm to the idea of producing it. All the equipment made me nervous and spending my afternoons editing at a computer seemed boring. But I was angry about something: the pervasive idea that a woman who wears "revealing" clothes is "asking for it." So I let myself be talked into making a radio piece on the subject. I don't know exactly what clicked as I started muddling my way through the piece. My tape wasn't that great, I struggled to fit clips together in a way that made sense, and the audio lab was still sterile and uninviting, but something hooked me. It might have been the moment in an interview as someone was telling a story and right as she said the word "doorbell," the doorbell rang. It seemed like something brilliant had happened, like all the sounds had fallen into place and were speaking for themselves. That was the first bit of tape that I couldn't bring myself to delete.

After that summer I helped start Youth Noise Network, an after-school youth radio program based at CDS. For the next four years I made pieces, hosted shows, and learned about radio. My first piece taught me the basics of editing. Another one taught me how to interview strangers and to always have extra batteries. At some point I learned about the FCC and figured out what an omnidirectional microphone was. But the piece that taught me the most—about storytelling, interviewing, and the power of youth radio—started with the audio equivalent of a severe case of writer's block. I was sixteen years old and slogging through my sophomore year of high school. I had a civics essay I needed to write, some chemistry homework I was putting off, and a Spanish test to study for; more importantly, though, I'd promised to have a piece ready for a radio show. I needed to produce something but no topic, person, or question held my attention long enough to get started. Finally I decided to revisit my first piece about clothes and the sexualization of women, but this time I wanted to talk to the girls who get called sluts in school and wear the kinds of clothes people associate with "asking for it."

First, I had to find people to interview, or the "dressy girls," as I and the rest of Youth Noise Network (YNN) came to call them. A fellow YNN-er suggested her usual lunch table as the place to start. A few days later when lunch time rolled around, I nervously headed to a part of the crowded, noisy cafeteria that I never ate in. I'd had a recorder squirreled away in my backpack all day, and I'd been trying to think of interview questions between classes. The cafeteria of my high school was kind of steamy and sticky like most high school cafeterias. It was also ugly, smelly, and full of background noise. I hovered at the end of the table where the four young women I wanted to interview were eating, gossiping, and trying to finish homework. I was wearing jeans and a very large sweatshirt that was quickly becoming an art project with its paint smears and patches. As soon as I sat down, an assistant principal came over to yell at us because we were using the chairs reserved for teachers. We moved. I'd lost my piece of paper with the questions on it. I had maybe twenty minutes to do this interview before the bell rang. "So," I began, "what are you wearing?"

The four of them immediately answer this question with precise descriptions of their outfits—brand names, V-necks, high-heeled flip flops. Yelling over the hundreds of hungry teenagers around us, I ask them why they're wearing what they're wearing, how they pick their clothes. It's a good thing I lost the prepared questions because there is no way I could have planned this interview better than it was spontaneously unfolding. Girls pick their jeans to make their butts look good, they tell me. It makes them feel good about themselves. Guys like it, too. Not only are clothes about attracting guys, they're about making other girls jealous. Jealous of your butt. Jealous of all the guys looking at it. And somehow: jealous so that they will want to be your friend.

We are sitting next to a handful of boys who are pretending they're not listening to this loud, blunt explanation of bodies, boys, and wardrobes. "What makes a guy look at you?" The dressy girls all pause and then in unison reply, "Skin, skank, skin. Lots of skin." Turning the microphone to the nearest boy, I ask if this is true. He mumbles agreement through a mouthful of food, and the girls laugh as if to say, "See? I told you so."

Skank, roughly defined by my interviewees as someone who walks around "with their thong hanging out," is not a word that you expect to hear on public radio. But that word, which is interchangeable with a whole lot of other words that you never hear on public radio, is part of stories that certainly should be heard. I know it's at least part of the stories of four teenagers I went to school with. The only problem is, no one is really talking to teens. For the most part, any discussion in the mainstream media about issues pertinent to young people—like clothes and self-esteem—is a discussion held among professors, sociologists, psychologists, and other "expert" adults. The voices of actual young people just aren't there. That's where youth radio producers like me come in.

HERE'S A BIT OF transcript from "Dressy Girls":

MELINA: I think to dress like a skank . . .

HOLLY, RACHEL, ARIELLE: Like Melina. Melina would know this.

MELINA: No, no. I think to dress like a skank is where you're wearing like a really, really, really, short, short skirt. And ummm, showing, like, having your thong hanging out and like, having your like breasts show . . .

ME: [quoting some *Seventeen* magazine summer fashion tips] Enhance
   bust; a pleated bodice adds fullness to your chest area.

MELINA: And wearing, like, really high heels, like that tall with a skirt and
   stuff.

RACHEL: Sounds familiar.

[laughter]

MELINA: I've never done that before.

HOLLY: Yeah, you have.

MELINA: No, I haven't! I'm serious! That was in sixth grade, that was in
   sixth grade!

ARIELLE: [laughing] Sixth grade and she was dressing like that. . . . So
   you admit, you admit it.

MELINA: I do, I admit that in sixth and seventh grade I dressed like a
   skank.

ME: The newest glasses, bikinis, and short shorts. Go for a miniskirt this
   season.

MELINA: Because I was ugly. I was really ugly in sixth and seventh grade.

HOLLY: Yeah, you were! Just kidding . . .

MELINA: And it boosted up my confidence.

ME: You thought other people would like you more because of the way
   you dressed?

MELINA: No, definitely not like me more but look at me more.

As a teenager, as a high school student, I had much easier access to other
youth. While making "Dressy Girls," my age definitely worked to my ad-
vantage in getting good interviews. I was less threatening as an interviewer
because I was the same age as the people I talked to, and we went to the
same school. I could interview them on their ground, at their cafeteria
table, but saw them in the hallways and in class every day, too.

That said, I didn't actually have that much in common with them besides age. I didn't pretend when I interviewed them that I did. I went into
the interviews wearing what I always wear with no pretension that at
some point we were going to be friends or sit around and dish about boys
and thongs. I was just curious about what they thought of their clothes,
themselves, and how others might see them. Up until this piece I had
mostly made pieces about myself; radio was a way of processing my own

experiences. I've discovered that lots of youth radio is exactly that, a way for producers to express themselves and tell their stories. However, I think youth radio tends toward pieces about self-discovery not because youth producers are shy or lazy, but because we've never had the opportunity to actually speak for ourselves in the media before. Just because no one is asking for our voices and stories doesn't mean we don't have them. I think the experience of feeling unrepresented, misrepresented, and unheard coupled with a teenager's desire to figure out and assert an identity is what motivates many youth producers to make pieces about themselves or their immediate communities. Strangely though, I think the same experiences make me, and perhaps other teen producers, capable of producing pieces about people that we don't know or have much in common with. I made "Dressy Girls" precisely because I saw that discussions about clothes, sex, self-image, and young women often lacked the voices of young women. Being tuned in to how I would want myself and my story portrayed on the radio helped me tell theirs, hopefully in a way that is honest and not judgmental. After all, discovering our connections to the world and to people who are different from us is also a part of growing up—and youth radio can be an important reminder for everyone to continue discovering, questioning, and extending themselves.

Now that I'm in college, I have no idea what the next four, five, or ten years will bring radio-wise, but I don't plan to stop listening anytime soon. I know youth radio will always be important to me, even when I am too old to be considered a youth producer. I'm interested in starting community radio stations, which I know almost nothing about. I'm interested in radio as a tool for language and culture preservation even though I know nothing about that either. My latest radio addiction is the Canadian Broadcasting Corporation. Obviously, I want to keep making radio pieces. Lots and lots of very experimental hour-and-a-half-long documentaries that no one will air except the amazing community-supported, solar-powered radio station in Canada that I'm going to start with a bunch of misfit teenagers.

Salt Is Flavor and Other Tips Learned While Cooking

Emily Botein

I CAME TO RADIO THROUGH FOOD. At age twelve I began cooking for a caterer, stuffing chicken breasts, baking chocolate chip cookies, and (this being the early 1980s) making pasta salad. After college I landed a job at the Quilted Giraffe, a four-star restaurant in New York. It was famous, among other things, for caviar beggar's purses. One of my daily tasks was filling crepes with a spoonful of caviar and a dollop of crème fraîche and then forming each one into a little bundle, tied with a chive bow.

Not a bad beginning for future years cleaning edits and nudging tape a tenth of a second at a time.

The restaurant closed after I had been there for a year. On unemployment, I took an internship at a public radio station. Next came my first paid radio job, on a National Public Radio series about food. We were still cutting tape with razor blades then; I had no real radio experience, but the woman who hired me said she knew I would be comfortable using my hands from years spent in a kitchen. She was right.

My Hands

Many years ago, I read an article in the *Boston Globe* about chefs and sous chefs. One chef described her sous chef as "my hands." That's how I want the people I produce—hosts, writers, reporters, guests—to think of me: I am their hands, an extension of their thoughts, their minds. Unlike most of the radio makers in this book, who often appear as narrators, I typically collaborate with someone else—a program host, a writer new to radio, or sometimes just my subject—who will be the voice and the face of the piece. I make the plans, nudge my collaborators through the process, and assemble the results. It's my job to make them sound good, which means different things to different people: Hosts want to sound smart; I want them to sound real and unguarded. I want to help them say what they

176

want to say, but I want them to speak more clearly, more leanly, and also more playfully than they might intend to. I want to make them sound as human as possible—with the nervousness and insecurities that implies.

1 + 1 = 3

I recently called up "the hands"—that sous chef from the *Boston Globe* article. I asked if she ever felt underappreciated in the kitchen. No, she said, but "I'm someone who always believes that 1 + 1 = 3." She knew that she and her chef were making better menus by bouncing ideas off each other. I like to think the same is true in radio.

In radio, plenty of people think producing other people is unsatisfying. They want to use their *own* words; they want to make their *own* statements. For me, working with other people is incredibly fulfilling. Someone is allowing me to get inside his or her brain. I feel like a conductor shaping the words to sound just as I want.

I am not a selfless, egoless producer. In fact, I am pretty controlling. And I think producing other people is just as much a job for control freaks as reporting a story is. Those of us who work from the sidelines may be even more controlling because we do it covertly—we're listening from outside the studio, behind the headphones, or on the other end of the phone line.

It's only worth it if you can take pleasure in the disguise—if you enjoy working in the control tower, manipulating the marionettes from backstage. You have to relish the host asking a question she only asked because you pointed her in that direction. You have to congratulate yourself that the ambient sound you recorded—the best ambi ever, which no one will ever notice, makes the piece sound so smooth that listeners can't help but be captivated. A producer has to celebrate the victories of the editing process—when, say, the reporter cuts a line of her writing, making the tape stronger and full of surprise.

Producing other people isn't *always* great. Plenty of times your pre-interview is better than what the host gets in the field. (If only you had done the interview! If only the host weren't such an idiot!) But when I'm producing someone else, I can only complain so much. It's the host's brain, but it's my "hands," and if they aren't working, I need to figure out why.

I like to work with people who have never done radio. In particular, I like to work with writers because they do something I don't: they write. We each bring something to the table, and if it works, we can make something together that neither of us would have been able to create on our own. Of course, working with writers can be a huge pain. I don't want them to do "books on tape"; I don't want them to cling to their words. If we're making radio, the end result is on my turf, not theirs. It's useful to let them know that from the start. What looks great on the page is often a snooze on the air.

As much as I might complain about the person I'm producing, it is actually a relief to work with someone else. It means I have to let go a little. There is only so much I can control. And in the end, that's part of the pleasure—I've thought about this piece, this topic, this interview so much that I may not see other, better, ways to produce the piece. If my hands have prepared him, a collaborator is more likely to feel he can detour from the roadmap I've laid out, and both of us may be surprised at the outcome, at a turn in a story that neither of us expected.

In the end, I need the other person as much as she needs me. She allows me to do my work—she gives me the ingredients, the tape, that I can play with later in the editing process. I can be a shy person, and my collaborator allows me to hide behind the tape. I don't want to hear myself behind the microphone. But I can't just be silent. My collaborator forces me to communicate what I want to hear, what kind of tape I want her to give me. Producing other people requires me to put into words what I want us to make together. And to be calm and clear about what I need: *It's triple-digit heat, but yes, our recording will sound better if you turn off the air conditioner.* When I listen back to some of my early interviews, I cringe as I hear myself unable to tell the guest where to sit. "Take control," I yell at the old tapes!

We're in the Weeds

When I started in a kitchen, what felt most foreign was the language. Someone told me to "fire" the scallops, and it felt like a TV show—we don't actually *say* "fire" for "cook," do we? But I remember the first time I called back, "Scallops fired!" and suddenly this world was mine. The starched white coat began to feel familiar, the clogs comfortable.

We have our own props in radio: recorders, microphones, and headphones. Some people complain about headphones—that they're cumbersome; that they make it harder to connect with the person being interviewed. But my headphones give me focus. I slip them on, and the rest of the world fades away.

Headphones can serve another purpose, too. One time I ended up lost in the field with a host. I had relied on MapQuest when I should have brought a map. We were doing an interview in a car. In a car? How will *that* sound, the guest, a literary academic, had asked me. Not great, I knew, but I wanted to convey a journey, and I wanted to take her back to a place where she'd lived many years before. She was skeptical but game. Which way did we want to go, she asked when we got in the car. Whichever way she wanted. Turned out, she didn't remember the way. I glanced at the MapQuest printout but knew it wasn't going to help much. So I kept my headphones on. The guest, who had been nervous about a radio interview in a car, realized she had to take charge. Forgetting her scholarly research, she became animated and started directing us—*Go this way. No this. Take a right. Oh, this is near where I used to live. No, maybe not.* She ended up having to call a friend to lead us out—all on tape. Now we've all gotten lost in a car; we weren't breaking any new ground. And did it serve the story? That's debatable. (My editor wasn't sure.) To my ears, it was a detour worth taking. The guest was lost; flustered, she suddenly became human. As a listener, that's when my ears perk up. I'm more likely to find her sympathetic, so I'm more likely to listen to what she has to say.

In that instance, my headphones served as a kind of protection—if I took them off, I'd end up nervous: after all, it's getting dark, and where are we? As a producer, I need to appear calm. The person I'm producing, or the guest who is waiting to be interviewed, doesn't need to know I'm not. What they need is a warm and focused face—assuring them everything is going entirely as planned—even when we're lost in the suburbs, or when the host hasn't shown up five minutes after the interview was supposed to start.

Of course, there are real accidents—like getting lost in the field—and then there are planned accidents.

I don't like to keep a lot from a host or someone I'm producing. Before we record, I try to go over in writing and in conversation what we are hoping to capture on tape. I want them to feel completely comfortable; I want them to think they know what's happening, to feel like they know just how things will unfold.

But I don't tell them everything.

(These are the planned accidents. The ones you keep in your back pocket, the questions you write down in shorthand that only you will understand. These are your little bits of ammunition to help you get the moments of surprise you yearn for.)

We're interviewing a musician. I happen to know she works in a high-end shoe store a couple of days a month. I want a tour of her shoe collection, but I know the host will be uncomfortable asking—what, after all, do shoes have to do with an up-and-coming music career? So I don't bring it up—until the end of the interview. I just slip it in—I whisper to the host— "we should do a tour of the closet." At that point, the interview has gone well, and he's willing. We see her vintage shoes as well as new ones; she proudly states, "I know shoes. I can talk about a lot of different lines." Bingo—a possible opener. As with the academic in the car, once we get the guest off what she thinks we want to talk about, she becomes the most animated. At last: the conversation she hasn't rehearsed in her head.

Mise en place

After spending time on radio shows and in restaurants, I think a kitchen, where a bad burn is a daily risk, enforces better habits than the perceived informality of a public radio program.

At the Quilted Giraffe, my day was spent preparing my mise en place, my set-up for service. I'd prep my vegetables, bone and smoke duck breasts, make pizza dough, pick thyme and tarragon, test sauces, make dressings. The work was routine, but I couldn't slip up. One-eighth-inch dice is just that—I'd square off the carrots or potatoes, I'd slice them into one-eighth-inch strips, then to one-eighth-inch batons, then to dice. My mise en place was often inspected before service; my sauces were tasted by the chef. I needed to be ready. If something was oversalted, I had to redo it. I couldn't hide. Prepping for dinner service feels a bit like doing the first edit on a radio piece. Either way, I'm naked—the least I can do is make sure my edits are clean, my intro drafted.

I'm not a particularly neat person; my desk is piled with junk. But when I'm editing audio, I try to approach my computer with the same sense of respect (and fear) I had for my *mise en place*. A mix on my digital editing software, Pro Tools, should be set up in a way that if someone else has to work on the piece, he can find what he needs quickly. For many people, these details seem petty and logistical—what do our Pro Tools habits reveal about our ability to create an artful narrative, after all? Well, my personal narrative may need help, and someone else may end up finishing my piece. Good habits enable better collaborations—and, hopefully, better radio at the end of the day.

Salt Is Flavor

Bruce, my colleague on the appetizer station, had many aphorisms. "The truth isn't always pretty" was one of his favorites. Another was "salt is flavor." It makes sense: sometimes salt is enough. You don't need to add a lot of spices and sauces if the food is good enough to speak for itself. The same is true in radio. It's easy to overedit tape.

It took me a long time to understand the value of a pause. When I listen to some of my first pieces, I want to add more space. Everything feels like it should be slower, have more time to breathe. Once an editor had me put an eight-second pause in a piece. I thought he was crazy. When I listen now, it doesn't seem long at all; it sounds the way people speak. Meaning, sometimes they don't. In an interview, there are usually moments of silence, and those moments can be powerful. Pauses break up the rhythm and add complexity. Pauses help us to listen better.

And just as the magic of a good meal can be its simplicity, I don't want to know how much work went into a radio piece. I may have had to record the narration five times and collect sixteen hours of tape for my six-minute piece, but that's my job. However heroic I may feel as a radio producer, as a listener, I don't need the details of what went into it. I don't want to be told how difficult it was to get an interview; just give me a good story. Make the menu simple—even if the prunes soaked for three months. What's important is the taste I get in the short amount of time I eat the dish. That's what will decide whether I'm still listening all the way through a five-minute radio segment.

It's Only Ears

I didn't work long enough in a restaurant kitchen to become a sous chef, but I did work long enough to know my job well. Sautéing foie gras each night allowed me to observe the smallest changes: the color of the meat, its touch under my finger. I knew what the middle would look like even before I sliced it open.

When I started out in radio, I logged a lot of tape. The woman who first hired me had me mark the stuff that stood out, to me. I was terrified by the task, but I remember she said, "It's only ears." She had many more years of experience than I did but she was curious to hear what interested me.

In radio, people always say, "Did you get good tape?" I remember being asked this after I had done my first few interviews—and I had no idea what to say. What was "good tape"? Would they like the same things that I do? There are times when good tape is universal—when both you and your editor point straight to the same moment—but there are also times when you'll have a difference of opinion. In a way, I hate the idea that there is this thing called "good tape," since of course it depends on what you *do* with the tape. But I also know the idea makes more sense the more you record. Good tape, to me, is the stuff that sounds (and is) spontaneous, accidental, slightly chaotic—like life. It takes time to trust your own instincts and, in particular, to tune your ears. When someone asks what to bring for dinner, I taste the entire meal in my head. I know just what will complement the rest of the menu. It has taken me a long time to be as confident about radio ingredients. And I'm still tasting.

Afterword

Listen

Jay Allison

WHEN I WAS SMALL, I was quiet. Not shy exactly, but not someone with a radio future either. My father, on the other hand, was a wonderful talker. A big man with a big personality, he was full of funny stuff and everyone enjoyed him, including me. There was no sense in trying to match his affable, amplified self. Instead, I watched and listened. A happy audience.

Growing up, my sisters and I were sheltered in the sense that my family spent time with other families like us. I suppose many families tend to keep to their own kind unless compelled to do otherwise, but we didn't branch out much or actively learn about different cultures, classes, or races. As a kid, it hardly occurred to me that there were other worlds out there, entirely other ways of thinking and being.

My school, too, was homogeneous, divided only by the customary cliques. I did not run with any particular crowd, standing at ease on the outside, observing. Not talking much.

Being unidentified with others kept me, in a way, unidentified to my-self. I think of it this way: I was a stranger to my own voice.

Some evenings, my father would get out the old Revere reel-to-reel tape recorder to make a family "radio" broadcast. He would perform the role of Master of Ceremonies and we children were invited to get in on the act as interviewees. The host was charming. The guests less so. I have old tapes with my giggles as my father introduced me, with continued giggles in response to every question. As I grew older, the recorded evidence proves that my stories remained inarticulate about the world or even my own life. I had nothing to say. I remember staring at the recording meter, an amber florescent eye blinking with each of my content-free utterances, a silent opening and closing, a measure of emptiness.

What stories did I have to tell? What voice would I use to tell them?

These questions persist fifty years later, after a career dedicated to answering them.

WHAT'S SO IMPORTANT ABOUT STORIES? The poet Muriel Rukeyser wrote, "The universe is made of stories, not of atoms." Stories define each of us. They have the power to divide or connect us as individuals and communities.

The earliest stories were told out loud. When we tell stories on the radio, we tap into a primitive and powerful human tradition, even an imperative, to speak and be heard, to compel listening.

Listen. What can you hear right now? How many sounds or voices? You may have tuned them out while you were reading, but you were receiving them. We are open and vulnerable to sound. A voice can sneak in, bypass the brain, and touch the heart. We are equally susceptible to the shout and the whisper, the threat and the plea. Voice contains breath and lives in time. So does radio.

For evidence of sound's primal power, I defer to Walter Murch, the godfather of film sound designers, writing on Transom.org. (We'll get to Transom later, but in brief it's a website dedicated to public radio storytelling, and I'll be quoting some of our guests):

> Hearing is the first of our senses to be switched on, four-and-a-half months after we are conceived. And for the rest of our time in the womb—another four-and-a-half months—we are pickled in a rich brine of sound that permeates and nourishes our developing consciousness: the intimate and varied pulses of our mother's heart and breath; her song and voice; the low rumbling and sudden flights of her intestinal trumpeting; the sudden, mysterious, alluring or frightening fragments of the outside world—all of these swirl ceaselessly around the womb-bound child, with no competition from dormant Sight, Smell, Taste or Touch.
>
> Birth wakens those four sleepyhead senses and they scramble for the child's attention—a race ultimately won by the darting and powerfully insistent Sight—but there is no getting around the fact that Sound was there before any of them, already waiting in the

womb's darkness as consciousness emerged, and was its tender midwife.

So although our mature consciousness may be betrothed to sight, it was suckled by sound, and if we are looking for the source of sound's ability—in all its forms—to move us more deeply than the other senses and occasionally give us a mysterious feeling of connectedness to the universe, this primal intimacy is a good place to begin.

Convinced? It's a little frightening, isn't it, to imagine that we are fooling around with such power? Yet most of what we hear on the radio does not wield it. If Murch has described a sonic theater of the air, the curtain is down.

IN THE MID-1970S, I had ended up in Washington, D.C., living in a friend's basement, which I shared with his dog. A few years before, I'd switched my college major from engineering to theater, with all the other changes that would imply.

The sixties and early seventies were fueled by a manic idealism and belief in the possibility of change, with young people spearheading that change. After school, I'd pursued that idea through theater, joining the experimental theater movement of the day, reading Grotowski, directing Brecht in storefronts, studying with children's theaters in the Soviet Union.

But the gas ran out. How do you make theatrical representations of life when you know so little of it? After a sheltered youth and education what was banked in the Life Experience Department? When I directed actors, what authority did I have to guide them? What stories did I know?

In a quandary, I pretty much dropped out during the time of basement living, until one evening a guy named Keith Talbot came over for dinner and told us about a new enterprise that had just started up down on M Street: National Public Radio. Keith was their quasi artist-in-residence, taking reel-to-reel recorders out into the field and creating Radio Experiences. This had a comforting theatrical ring to it, but it was connected to reality, to the world. I liked the sound of it. I liked the sound of the mission statement, too, penned by Bill Siemering.

National Public Radio will serve the individual: it will promote personal growth; it will regard the individual differences among men with respect and joy rather than derision and hate; it will celebrate the human experience as infinitely varied rather than vacuous and banal; it will encourage a sense of active constructive participation, rather than apathetic helplessness. . . .

The total service should be trustworthy, enhance intellectual development, expand knowledge, deepen aural esthetic enjoyment, increase the pleasure of living in a pluralistic society and result in a service to listeners which makes them more responsive, informed human beings and intelligent responsible citizens of their communities and the world.

In fact, this language was addictive to a hopeful young idealist searching for purpose and identity. Organizations should be careful when they write their mission statements, because good ones will attract zealots, and they're tough to get rid of. They don't like having their dreams betrayed by pragmatists. They want the mission honored because they've pinned their own life's meaning upon it. As the writer and radio maker/critic Sarah Vowell posted on Transom, "I still believe in public radio's potential. Because it's the one mass medium that's still crafted almost entirely by true believers."

Keith loaned me one of NPR's Sony 800B recorders and enough five-inch reels of audio tape to get started. NPR had no security system in those days. There was a street-level entrance near the elevators on M Street, and I just walked in every day, grabbed supplies, asked for advice from the engineers and producers, found an empty edit booth, and went to work. No one particularly cared or even knew that I wasn't employed there. The more, the merrier. The enterprise was inventing itself, as was I.

For years after that, I traveled all over, emerging from a sheltered past, encountering every kind of person I could. Carrying the passport of a microphone, I had permission to ask questions about anything. I could satisfy any curiosity and hear about unfamiliar lives. Afterward, with razor blades and multiple tape recorders, I cut and mixed the voices and sounds and brought some of the "infinitely varied" stories to air.

Theatrical training was useful. Radio is, after all, a performance art, its stories told in time, complete with scene, character, and conflict, needing rhythm, pacing, climax to hold interest. There was no established NPR style yet, so inventiveness was the order of the day. Lots of highs, lots of lows. Many voices. For my part, I was discovering my own voice by listening to the voices of others and passing them on.

Ever since then, I've been trying to repay that original loan of a tape recorder, to infect others with enthusiasm for the mission of public radio, and to create street-level entrances. I want to extend the same invitation that was extended to me.

"YOU HEAR STUFF YOU HAVEN'T HEARD BEFORE, from a stranger or from someone you know, and you think, 'Yeah, I am connected.' I think that's the goal, the responsibility, the challenge of public radio."

"What would your ideal radio day be?"

"I'd want the human voice expressing grievances, or delight, or whatever it might be. But something real."

That's Studs Terkel in conversation on Transom. For many of us, Studs represents the ideal of listening. He was interested in *everyone*. He was a story-gatherer, a populist, a curious mind, an educator, and a theatrical presence—all qualities that feed the mission of public radio.

Public radio began life as primarily an "educational" enterprise. Many early licensees were universities, and programming was often that deemed Good for You. As we moved into news, we provided an "alternative" service, partly out of necessity—there wasn't enough money (or listeners) to be anything else! As other radio networks have abandoned serious news, public radio has become the primary news source for millions of Americans. No longer an alternative, it often only echoes its original educational imperative and even some portions of its mission.

Yet public radio depends on the passion of its listeners. What other enterprise, besides church, depends for its survival on users paying for what they can get for free? News on public radio is vital to many, but the passion arises from a different source. Bill Siemering again on Transom: "Radio is a companion that makes the everyday elegant, like a Shaker chair or carved wooden spoons. It's with you when you're making breakfast, nursing the baby, fixing the car, sewing, or driving (even a tractor). Radio is personal, for both the producer and listener. This is why it has such power and why we feel so passionate about it. Hearing a voice alone gives radio an intimacy unmatched by any other medium. And because public radio is non-commercial we establish a bond with our listeners through our art."

From Transom, the writer and radio aficionado John Hodgman: "Where television luridly reveals everything, radio is coy; radio conceals its sources. It is a voice behind a curtain, and you must provide the face. Or, if you do not keep your radio behind a curtain, as I do, you can imagine it as voices in the next room. This is what makes radio so power-fully consoling to the lonely—it creates the illusion of company in a way that few other media can. Public radio is particularly adept at creating this illusion of companionship . . . because of the close and uncanny natural-ness of its voices."

We are blind listening to the radio. Our imaginations are in play. We create the characters, envision the settings. Images are indelible because we participate in their creation.

Listening to the radio is listening to a person. Radio stations or net-works are like people. They have personalities. That's what, as a listener, you are responding to—sensibility, tone, personality. Here is the Cape Cod artist Dennis Downey on Transom for the anniversary of Marconi's first transatlantic transmission from Cape Cod: "Even if the distance is very far, or . . . if the story told is very large, you talk like you're talking to one person at a time. . . . Radio goes out in all directions within a circle, to be heard, altogether at once. . . . But the words fall from the sky and into the ears of always one person at a time."

TEN YEARS AFTER STARTING in radio in Washington, I had ended up in Woods Hole, Massachusetts. There was no public radio up here on Cape Cod, Martha's Vineyard, and Nantucket, and I began to dream of a radio station with a personality, not just of one person, but a whole community —one that built on the broad mission of public radio and sounded like a place, built from the voices of the people who lived there.

It took about ten years of grassroots work to do it, a struggle I'd not recommend to any but the fanatical, but we finally ended up with our own Cape and Islands public radio station. Our service was adopted by WGBH in Boston who shared our commitment to serve the local commu-nity. We carry the usual NPR fare, and have a small but strong local news service, but we also have something called "Sonic IDs," an inside working title that stuck.

These are thirty- to ninety-second fragments of life here, each one ending with the station call letters—stories, memories, oral histories, overheard conversations, jokes, poems, minidocumentaries—all told by our neighbors. In fact, that's the word that describes the station at its best: neighborly. Of course, we don't all know each other, but we have one thing in common: this place.

Our Sonic IDs come on randomly, amid the news of the day. Suddenly, following a news report, someone begins telling you about his grandfather trying to get a cow on a sailboat, or a homeless woman talks of finding places to sleep in a resort community, or a kid recites a little poem, and the effect is uncanny. You feel your local life moving in parallel with the life of the world. It's almost as if there's been a mistake, something unplanned, that an actual person, your neighbor, jumped up and commandeered the electronics. In that instant, there's a moment that's real, unexpectedly, and a connection is made. The measure of success is this: when one of these little stories comes on, you turn and look at the radio.

There is also *hope* in these stories, even a utopian hope for more empathy and harmony. A community is like the world. We share the space, but we don't necessarily know each other. Here, like everywhere, we are parochial, often distrustful. People from one island tend to think they're generally superior to people from the other island. But if you're a Nantucketer, and you hear a good story from a fisherman, say, and you like the guy telling it and laugh with him, and then discover at the end that he's from Martha's Vineyard, you may have to adjust your worldview. There is great power in shared stories, in these seacoast towns and around the world, and in the invitation to share them.

Along with Sonic IDs, we constantly experiment with other ways to ask listeners to become the *content* of the station. We loan out tape recorders, keep a listener line for stories, and generally invite people to bring their voices to the air. One person who took us up was Carol Wasserman:

Imagine that you are a young woman who has made several unfortunate choices, and finds herself alone with her child on the hardscrabble coast of Massachusetts. Without a clue what to do next.

You will take a succession of meaningless jobs, for little money. State law requires an employer to provide health insurance to those who work twenty hours a week. You will be hired to work nineteen. You will spend your life providing the Department of Transitional Assistance with photocopies of your pitiful bank statement and your electricity bills and—frequently—copies of your medical records. So that anyone might answer for themselves the question which you have asked yourself over and over and over, namely: "What is *wrong* with you?"

There is nothing wrong with you, but you don't know that yet. You spend your evenings with the radio on, listening to the voices in the darkness. You spend your days in a factory, counting things into piles of ten as they pass in front of you on a conveyor belt. But when you get home, public radio is there to tell you what happened while you were gone.

This is where the invitation came in. Carol brought a typed essay to the station—a lovely one, about the hard life in a resort town after Labor Day. We produced it and then many more from her in subsequent years. She became a regular on *All Things Considered* nationally, and listening to her own voice coming over the radio she was, as she said, amazed at the woman she had become. "But all you have become is part of the achingly important institution of public radio. Which pulled you from deep water and into the boat. Which gave you a voice, and surprised you with the news that there is nothing wrong with you at all, except that you had not yet told your stories . . . not yet learned to accept the invitation which public radio has always extended to all of us. To listen. And, if we will, speak up."

When the radio station first signed on, the transmitter was switched and silence cleaned out the static, and the first word to emerge from the silence was "Listen."

AT ATLANTIC PUBLIC MEDIA, the founding organization for the radio station, we pursue all kinds of ways to extend the mission of public radio by opening the door to citizen participation.

Through series like *The Sonic Memorial Project* and *Hidden Kitchens* (collaborations with the Kitchen Sisters) we've called out to listeners to contribute, to send us the sounds and stories they hold precious. Our first project like that, Lost & Found Sound, made it clear that sonic artifacts carry a special kind of power. People sent sounds that brought the past alive for them—clinking milk bottles, porch door slams, trolley cars. And they sent us the voices of their loved ones who had passed away, often with a note like "it's all I have left," as if the voice was something *actual*, a vestige, with a kind of ghostly energy. People don't have this kind of relationship with photographs. Those can be kept at arm's length. Voices go inside. In hearing your mother's voice, she becomes, in a way, my mother, and I am drawn back to my own history and outward into yours. Each listener's sonic artifact triggered response from other listeners, who sent in their old audio, and a kind of community memory was built.

Our series *This I Believe* asked listeners to share something even more intimate, their fundamental convictions. More than 65,000 essays were sent in. It was a nonhomogeneous group, to say the least, from all over the world and represented an astonishing spectrum of belief. At its root, this series was about listening. There was no opportunity for rebuttal or argument. The only response was to write one of your own, to contribute your own voice to the commons. One of our essayists, Ted Gup, said: "If you take all the essays in the aggregate, what you have is sort of a national anthem. That's the beauty of it: You have a multiplicity of voices and it's a celebration of that multiplicity."

It's the many strains of that anthem I long to hear on public radio. At APM, our invitation to sing along extends to the Internet.

In the 1980s, I frequented something called the WELL, an early experiment in online community started by the people at Whole Earth in San Francisco. The phone bill to log on with my 300-baud modem from Woods Hole, Massachusetts, was staggering. But it felt like time traveling to the future, and in a way, it was. I hosted the radio forum on the WELL, but when my eldest daughter got caught up in a bad medical situation, I turned to the WELL for support. This was an unheard of phenomenon at the time—seeking community with virtual strangers. Most people hadn't even heard of "email" and the web, as such, didn't exist, but pioneering outposts like the WELL proved that this way of connecting was real. I felt like public radio could learn from it. Radio, after all, is disembodied communication among strangers.

Whole Earth has as its credo "Access to tools, ideas, and practice." Those are the principles on which we founded Transom.org. And to that list we add "mission." Transom tells you what microphone to buy and how to use it, but more than that we try to pass the baton, to attract a new generation of zealots, bred on the Internet, to bring their talents to public radio. Remarkable guests present manifestos and answer questions. We feature new work from new people. Our premise is that if we don't attract passionate talent, we wither. Creative people are generally drawn not by money, but by community, welcoming peers, and an appreciative audience. The people we want to guide us into the future need to value our roots in public service, but also know the ways to penetrate public consciousness in a new era of information delivery.

From Transom.org sprang PRX, the Public Radio Exchange (prx.org). This concept began in a Transom article I subversively titled "The Interested Stations Group," implying that any station not part of this group was "uninterested." The idea was to create an Internet repository for the voices we're not hearing. Public radio stations could browse the stacks and place this work in time slots saved for adventure and risk. Citizens could have direct access to local markets where their stories would be heard. A new category of employee would emerge, the PRX Jockey, who would act as the listener's agent, finding the best stuff for each community's audience. We would put the public back in public radio.

In collaboration with the Station Resource Group, we actually built the thing, working originally with programmers in Russia. The site has grown over the years and is quite remarkable—an amazing tool employed in all sorts of creative ways by the PRX staff, producers, stations, and the populace. It is open to all, welcomes peer review, and houses the largest body of critical writing on radio in existence. The fact is, thousands of individual voices are now on the PRX, speaking in their own styles, pushing edges freely, available to any station that is, well, . . . interested.

THE WORLD IS A NOISY PLACE; every day it gets noisier with content. How do you choose what to hear? Do you want what is familiar, something comforting in the chaos? Or do you want something surprising to wake you up? Here is the writer Rick Moody posting on Transom: "While I admire what public radio is and has been trying to do for twenty-five years or more, I find that I have also come to disbelieve it somehow, for the simple reason that I cannot believe that all of human life and psychology, all of human events, all of human history (not to mention the lives and environment of our animal friends), can always be rendered in exactly the same way. Suddenly, a medium that I love, that is, because I love thinking with my ears, begins to seem deeply suspect to me."

At Transom and PRX, we are looking for new voices and new ways of telling. We hope to embrace a greater range of style; we don't impose an expectation of how someone should sound or how a story should be told. Some pieces may not ever make it to public radio because they are too far out of an accepted existing style. Still, it's important to explore those boundaries and to talk about what makes the cut in public radio and what doesn't, and, more importantly, why. From Transom, the editor and host of On the Media, Brook Gladstone:

> Here's what I like about most public radio news magazines. The reporting is solid, the subjects are important and relevant, and the level of discourse is high. The audience is respected. These are the keys to public radio's success. While more and more news outlets slice up consistently smaller pieces of the audience pie, public radio consistently gains listeners, so it's doing something right.
>
> Here, in my humble opinion, is what's wrong: As they become the primary news source for more and more Americans, public radio newsmagazines are restricting their own ability to move listeners. Like physicians in medieval times they seek to balance the four humors (so as not to be too choleric, sanguine, phlegmatic or melancholy) by blood-letting. Public radio newsmagazines are looking a little pallid these days, because the passion has been drained off.

On public radio we need to hear the news, investigative journalism, solid reporting, no one questions that. But the more we regularize our sound in the name of reliability, the more we lull our audience. Any break from established style begins to seem jarring, not exciting.

You generally listen to two kinds of stories: those you need to hear and those you want to hear. Radio news generally assumes the information is something you need. The other kind of story is more mysterious. It may be something you want to hear, but don't *know* you want to hear. It is not predictable, searchable. It is accidental, having a quality of ambush. It is one person speaking to another, and falls outside the realm of perceived need. One champion of the individual voice is the reporter Robert Krulwich, speaking here at Third Coast International Audio Festival to an audience of producers and reporters. "Even if you're working in an organization which doesn't want you to be personal, which wants you to sound like the others, the secret thing you do is you sound sort of like the others, but you put in a little bit of your heart somewhere in there . . . just a little. And if it's there, it's like a marker. It's the IOU to your soul. And sometimes they let you sing loudly. And sometimes you have to sing soft. But you keep singing. You never ever stop."

There is something odd about those who want to tell stories on the radio. What sort of person wants to whisper in your ear from far away? What sort wants to be intimate, while remaining utterly detached, even disembodied? Who is drawn to sending an invisible voice through the invisible air in all directions to everyone?

The fact that we are odd is significant, because it can be used to resist the regularization that happens in every bureaucracy and organization. Oddness is what constitutes individuality.

WHEN I WAS SMALL I was quiet, but that didn't take away the wish to participate.

As for my own voice, some days, I recognize it as authentic. But it feels amplified when it is joined by the voices of others. It is in wielding the strange power of sound, in sharing the mission of public radio, and in trying to honor Studs Terkel's plea for "something real" that I feel most myself.

There are our stories, and there are everyone else's. When we use our voices to tell the stories of others, something may be gained in consistency of style, efficiency, and journalistic credibility, but something is lost too. When we let the other voices speak for themselves, we hear a public radio as astonishing as the world itself.

Perhaps we can find ways to lend a little of *all* of our voices to the air, just to remind us that we're all here and that we're neighbors.

Public radio will be as inclusive and representative as we demand it to be. Its anthem will be sung by as many as will join the chorus. Public radio will be as strong as we make it—not as professionals, but as citizens who view the public conversation as a collective opportunity and a responsibility, who remember that the invitation is always there: "To listen. And, if we will, speak up."

About the Contributors

JAD ABUMRAD is the host and producer of WNYC's *Radio Lab*, an award-winning radio series that explores big ideas through conversation, sound, and storytelling. The son of a scientist and a doctor, he did most of his growing up in Tennessee, before studying creative writing and music composition at Oberlin College in Ohio. Following graduation, Abumrad wrote music for films, and reported and produced documentaries for a variety of local and national public radio programs.

JAY ALLISON is one of public radio's most honored producers. He was the host and curator of *This I Believe* on National Public Radio. Over the last thirty years, he has independently produced hundreds of documentaries and features for radio and television, and has won virtually every major industry award, including five Peabodys. He co-created the acclaimed websites Transom.org, which helps people tell their own stories, and the Public Radio Exchange (prx.org), which helps get those stories on the radio. Allison also founded the public radio station for Martha's Vineyard, Nantucket, and Cape Cod, where he lives. With his friends the Kitchen Sisters, Allison co-produced and curated the NPR series *Lost & Found Sound*, the post-9/11 *Sonic Memorial Project*, and *Hidden Kitchens*. His ongoing project *Life Stories* gives tape recorders to citizens and helps them tell about their lives. Allison is now bringing the live storytelling project The Moth to public radio.

DAMALI AYO is an artist, writer, performer, and clothing designer. According to ayo, "art should make you think and feel." Much of her Now Art is participatory and free; she eschews art that is primarily for decoration or profit. She believes that artists' true place is at the forefront of social change movements. In 2003 ayo created the internationally acclaimed web-art-performance rent-a-negro.com, which explores the commodification of race and the interactions between blacks and whites in society. Her book,

How to Rent a Negro, was lauded as "one of the most trenchant and amusing commentaries on contemporary race relations" and received an honorable mention in the Outstanding Book Awards from the Gustavus Myers Center for the Study of Bigotry and Human Rights in 2005.

The radio feature "Living Flag: Panhandling for Reparations," which ayo co-produced with Dmae Roberts, won a 2005 Silver Reel Award from the National Federation of Community Broadcasters.

JOHN BIEWEN is audio program director at the Center for Documentary Studies at Duke University. His radio reporting and documentary work has taken him to forty American states and to Europe, Japan, and India. Biewen started as a reporter with Minnesota Public Radio. He reported for NPR News from the Midwest and the Rocky Mountains, and then spent eight years as a correspondent/producer with American RadioWorks, the documentary unit of American Public Media. Among other honors, Biewen's work has received two Robert F. Kennedy Memorial Awards for coverage of the disadvantaged, the Scripps Howard National Journalism Award, and the Third Coast International Audio Festival's Public Service Award. He teaches undergraduates and continuing studies students in CDS's Certificate in Documentary Studies program.

EMILY BOTEIN, an independent radio producer based in New York, helped launch Public Radio International's *The Next Big Thing* in 1999 and served as its senior producer. Since 2005, she has been involved with a range of shows and institutions, including *American Routes*, the Australian Broadcasting Corporation, NPR, Nextbook.org, *Studio 360*, and *Weekend America*. Before going into radio, Botein worked for seven years on local and national folklore programming initiatives at the Smithsonian Institution, the Brooklyn Arts Council, and the Center for Traditional Music and Dance. Before that, she received a professional pastry certificate from Tante Marie's Cooking School and made appetizers at a four-star restaurant in New York City.

CHRIS BROOKES was a theater director before he became a radio journalist. During the 1980s he reported out of war zones in Central America, and was a field documentary producer for the Canadian network radio program *CBC Sunday Morning*. More recently, as an independent radio producer, his documentaries have won international awards including a Peabody and a

Prix Italia, and have been broadcast in the United States, Ireland, Australia, New Zealand, the Netherlands, Austria, Finland, Sweden, Canada, and Britain. He has directed and produced documentaries for Canadian network television, and his television writing has been nominated for a Gemini Award. A published author and playwright, Brookes has taught documentary feature making and storytelling at radio festivals and workshops across North America and Europe. As a sound artist, his audio art has been exhibited at international festivals and released on CD. Brookes currently directs the production company Battery Radio with studios at the bottom of the cliff where Marconi received the first transatlantic wireless message in St. John's, Newfoundland.

SCOTT CARRIER is an independent radio producer and writer who lives in Salt Lake City, Utah. His radio stories have been broadcast on *All Things Considered*, *Day to Day*, *This American Life*, and *Weekend America*. His print stories have been published in *Harper's*, *Esquire*, *GQ*, and *Mother Jones*. A collection of stories, *Running after Antelope*, was published in March 2001 by Counterpoint. Some of his radio stories can be heard on hearingvoices.com.

KATIE DAVIS is a writer and broadcaster living in Washington, D.C. She is a regular commentator for NPR's *All Things Considered* and a contributor to PRI's *This American Life*. She is the founder/director of the Urban Rangers, which mentors teenagers and raises money for their college educations. Davis has released a three-CD set of her work over the past decade called *Neighborhood Stories*. She is currently at work on a memoir based on these stories.

SHERRE DELYS has worked with some of her favorite writers and musicians to create radio art that finds a true meeting between sound and story. Her work has been commissioned by national broadcasters and artist-run Internet stations and presented at major museums and cultural centers in Europe, America, and Australasia. She has enjoyed teamwork as a producer for *The Listening Room* at the Australian Broadcasting Corporation (ABC) and for *The Next Big Thing* at WNYC. She has collaborated with visual artists and architects on sound installations for the Sydney Olympics and Biennale of Sydney, and has worked with sculptor Joan Grounds for more than a decade —their sound sculptures enter into a call-and-response with the environments they inhabit. DeLys has also performed with improvising music groups, created sound designs for Sydney Theatre Company, hosted conversations with musicians for ABC TV, and taught and published on sound art and documentary. More recently she founded Pool, ABC's first participatory media project. As executive producer, DeLys works with researchers, radio producers, and the Pool community of contributors to develop new forms of collaborative creation in public media online.

LENA ECKERT-ERDHEIM helped found the Center for Documentary Studies' Youth Noise Network in 2003 and worked with YNN throughout high school. She graduated from Durham School of the Arts in 2007 and now attends Smith College.

IRA GLASS is the host and creator of the public radio program *This American Life*. The show had its premiere on Chicago's public radio station WBEZ in 1995 and is now heard on more than 500 public radio stations each week by over 1.8 million listeners. In March 2007 a television adaptation of *This American Life* premiered on the Showtime cable network. Glass began his career as an intern at NPR's network headquarters in Washington, D.C., in 1978, when he was nineteen years old. For the next seventeen years, he worked on the daily NPR network news programs, first as an editor and producer, and later on air, as a reporter and host. Under Glass's editorial direction, *This American Life* has won the highest honors for broadcasting and journalistic excellence, including the Peabody and duPont-Columbia awards. In 2007 he edited a collection of narrative journalism, *The New Kings of Nonfiction*, published by Riverhead Books.

ALAN HALL has been producing radio broadcasts since 1990 and has built an international reputation for long-form features, music programming, and what's been called "impressionistic radio." Much of his work has been produced for the BBC, but he has also had programs commissioned by the Australian Broadcasting Corporation ("Once Around Joby Talbot"), Danish Radio ("Tin Pan Alley"), and Chicago's WBEZ ("Studs Terkel—The Last Touch"). Hall's non-broadcast work includes the production of numerous audio tours for art galleries and museums and running the Creative Radio segment of Goldsmiths College's MA Radio Course (1998 to present). His programs have received many awards, including two coveted Prix Italias,

Prix Bohemia and Third Coast International Audio Festival awards, and several Sony Radio Academy Awards.

NATALIE KESTECHER has been an on-staff feature maker in the Features and Performance Unit of the Australian Broadcasting Corporation for the last seven years. Her first degree was in history and drama, with further studies in communications and scriptwriting. Before finding radio, Kestecher taught English to migrants in Australia and Spaniards in Spain, edited a disability journal, worked in a youth detention center, and sold lots of shoes. She's recently also fulfilled a lifelong ambition of becoming a marriage celebrant. These skills have proved invaluable in her media career. She blends fixation, fate, fact, and fiction to create unusual stories that demonstrate the fluid form and boundless possibilities of the radio medium.

THE KITCHEN SISTERS (Davia Nelson and Nikki Silva) are producers of the duPont-Columbia Award–winning and James Beard Award–nominated NPR series *Hidden Kitchens*, and the two Peabody Award–winning NPR series, *Lost & Found Sound* and *The Sonic Memorial Project*. *Hidden Kitchens*, heard on *Morning Edition*, explores the world of secret, unexpected, below-the-radar cooking across America—how communities come together through food. The series inspired their first book, *Hidden Kitchens: Stories, Recipes, and More from NPR's The Kitchen Sisters*, a *New York Times* Notable Book of the Year for 2005, which was also nominated for a James Beard Award for Best Writing on Food. Their national radio collaborations, in partnership with Jay Allison, have brought together independent producers, artists, writers, archivists, and public radio listeners throughout the country to create richly layered, highly produced, intimate, and provocative radio documentaries that chronicle untold stories of American culture and traditions.

MARIA MARTIN is a pioneering public radio journalist with over two dozen awards for her work covering U.S. Latino issues and Latin America. She began her radio career as a volunteer at the first Latino-owned and -operated public radio station in the country—KBBF in Santa Rosa, California. She's gone on to develop groundbreaking programs and series for public radio, including NPR'S *Latino USA*, and *Después de las Guerras: Central America after the Wars*. A recipient of a Fulbright and three Knight fellowships, she has extensive experience in journalism and radio training in Latin America, especially in Guatemala and Bolivia. Martin holds a master's degree in journalism from the Ohio State University, and currently heads the GraciasVida Center for Media and GraciasVida Productions based in Austin, Texas, and Antigua, Guatemala.

KAREN MICHEL is an independent radio producer who got her start in media as a guest on Art Linkletter's *Kids Say the Darndest Things*. Based in upstate New York, she has lived and worked in Alaska, Mexico, Japan, Greenland, India, Canada, Kenya, Nepal, Madagascar, and other geographies real and imagined. Michel works regularly with teen radio groups (notably WNYC's multi-award-winning Radio Rookies), teaches workshops around the country, and continues to produce work for national radio programs. She is also a photographer, and is interested in developing "performance documentary," combining visuals, text, and sound. She has numerous awards (including a Peabody) and fellowships from the Robert Wood Johnson Foundation, the National Endowment for the Arts, the Corporation for Public Broadcasting, the National Federation of Community Broadcasters, the Japan Foundation, and the Fulbright/Indo-U.S. Subcommission.

RICK MOODY's first novel, *Garden State* (1992), was the winner of the Editor's Choice Award from the Pushcart Press. His novel *The Ice Storm* (1994) was made into a film directed by Ang Lee in 1997. His other books include two collections of short fiction, *The Ring of Brightest Angels around Heaven* and *Demonology*; the novels *Purple America* and *The Diviners*; a book of novellas, *Right Livelihoods*; and *The Black Veil: A Memoir with Digressions*, which won the PEN/Martha Albrand Award for the Art of the Memoir. He is a past recipient of the Addison Metcalf Award, the *Paris Review* Aga Khan Prize, and a Guggenheim fellowship. His radio pieces have appeared on *The Next Big Thing* and at the Third Coast International Audio Festival.

JOE RICHMAN is an award-winning independent producer and reporter for NPR's *All Things Considered* and the founder of the production company Radio Diaries. Since the 1990s Radio Diaries has helped pioneer a model for working with people to document their own lives. Past series and programs include *Teenage Diaries*, *Prison Diaries*, *New York Works*, "My So-

Called Lungs," "Mandela: An Audio History," and "Thembi's AIDS Diary." Richman is also an adjunct professor at Columbia University's Graduate School of Journalism.

DMAE ROBERTS is a two-time Peabody Award–winning independent radio artist and writer, who has written and produced more than four hundred audio art pieces and documentaries for NPR and PRI programs. Her work is often autobiographical or about cross-cultural peoples and is informed by her biracial identity. Her documentary "Mei Mei, a Daughter's Song" is a harrowing account of her mother's childhood in Taiwan during World War II. She led the production of *Crossing East*, the first Asian American history series on public radio. Roberts received the 2007 Dr. Suzanne Ahn Award for Civil Rights and Social Justice from the Asian American Journalists Association and was one of fifty artists selected for the 2007 United States Artist Rockefeller Fellowship. Her other awards include the Robert F. Kennedy Journalism Award, the Casey Medal, the United Nations Silver Award, two Clarion Awards, two Heart of America Awards, and the National Lesbian and Gay Journalists Award. Roberts is the executive producer of MEDIARITES, a nonprofit organization dedicated to multicultural arts production in radio and educational outreach.

STEPHEN SMITH is executive editor of American RadioWorks, the documentary unit of American Public Media. Smith reports on a wide range of international and domestic issues, including human rights, science and health, race relations, and American history. Smith is the coeditor of *Say It Plain: A Century of Great African American Speeches* (New Press, 2007). Smith has won the duPont–Columbia University Gold Baton, for investigative reporting in the Balkans, as well as many other national journalism awards. Smith graduated from Macalester College in St. Paul, Minnesota, and was a William Benton Fellow at the University of Chicago, where he earned a master's degree in the humanities.

SANDY TOLAN has reported on land, water, identity, and conflict from more than thirty-five countries. He is the author of two books, including *The Lemon Tree*, a finalist for a 2006 National Book Critics Circle award. Tolan has written for dozens of newspapers and magazines, and produced hundreds of reports and documentaries for NPR and other public radio networks. His work has been recognized with more than two dozen national and international awards. He is co-founder of Homelands Productions, for twenty years the producer of international documentary programming for public radio. Most recently Tolan has been senior producer for WORKING, an international series of worker profiles aired on *Marketplace*, and for *The Hunger Chronicles*, a series for public radio and the web. Tolan is associate professor of journalism at the Annenberg School at the University of Southern California, where he teaches radio documentary, magazine writing, and multimedia reporting classes.

Editor's Note

Hearing the Documentaries

THE ESSAYISTS in *Reality Radio* were asked to do a hard thing: describe a sonic craft for the mute page. It's an enterprise that could bring to mind the line, probably first uttered by Elvis Costello, "Writing about music is like dancing about architecture. It's a really stupid thing to want to do." Clearly, I don't think it's stupid to write about documentary radio or music. (For that matter, a dance about architecture is something I'd like to see.) But throughout the book our contributors describe and explicate radio pieces, and those pieces ought to be heard. Rather than include with the book a CD that could hold only short audio slices from nineteen producers, we've posted samples of our essayists' works on a website. There you can hear substantial excerpts and complete works by the *Reality Radio* contributors, including, of course, the pieces described in these pages. The site also offers links to more audio documentary work, by our essayists and other producers—including podcasts. Please visit the book's companion website at www.realityradiobook.org.

Acknowledgments

REALITY RADIO had its beginnings a number of years ago when Iris Tillman Hill, longtime book editor at the Center for Documentary Studies, floated the question. Would I be interested in developing a book exploring contemporary documentary radio? Well, I replied, the world could certainly use one. By the end of that first brief conversation, we'd agreed on a general vision for this book. Iris provided indispensable guidance from start to end.

My colleague Alexa Dilworth, the current book editor at CDS (and a keen radio listener), was my day-to-day partner, sounding board, and co-editor. Thankfully, we agreed on almost everything. Alexa's intelligence, skill, and friendship made this a truly enjoyable journey. Her contributions appear on every page.

The leadership of the Center for Documentary Studies, especially Tom Rankin and Lynn McKnight, "got" Reality Radio and its value from the beginning. The book would not exist without their support. Our attempt to celebrate the broadest range of nonfiction audio work, from journalism to edgy art, reflects CDS's welcome-all-comers sensibility.

David Perry, editor in chief at the University of North Carolina Press, embraced Reality Radio enthusiastically, which meant everything. David and his colleagues made observations about the manuscript that helped us to hone the book significantly.

On several levels, the book bears the fingerprints of Johanna Zorn and Julie Shapiro of the Third Coast International Audio Festival. Early on, they cheered our plans and pledged to help spread the word among radiophiles. Julie suggested several potential essayists, people who weren't on our initial lists but have greatly enhanced the final product. More broadly, the Third Coast impresarias have done much to nurture the creative nonfiction audio that Reality Radio celebrates. They've championed new and innovative voices in this country and introduced the American radio community to brilliant feature makers from abroad—including the four international contributors whose essays appear here.

Our special thanks to Jay Allison, who among many other things, is the founder of Transom.org. Several of *Reality Radio*'s essays—those by Scott Carrier, Ira Glass, and the Kitchen Sisters—were adapted from or built upon "Manifestos" first written for Transom.

I'm grateful to David Haas for his generous financial contribution, which helped us launch the book—and remunerate these chronically underpaid artists for their work on these essays.

Radio producers are comfortable in varying degrees with the task of writing for the page about their audio creations. I'm indebted to the book's contributors for taking on the challenge, and for tolerating the editor(s). These essayists wrote with all the skill, care, and passion they bring to radio, and for that we're all lucky.

Finally, and above all, I thank my wife, Jodi Halweg Biewen, and my children, Harper and Lucas. I adore my work—making radio and teaching radio—and that work often takes me away from my family. They love me anyway, and I love them more than anything in the whole wide world.